MY

BOOK

Large Print

Personal Planning & Reflection

Paula Nafziger

Title............................. MY BOOK Large Print
Subtitle .... Personal Planning & Reflection
Version.......................... Paperback, Large Type 18 point
Author .... Paula Nafziger, Chaplain
Subject Heading............. Mind & Body/Spirituality
ISBN-13 978-1948136754

Buy-1 Give-1 When you buy this book, one will be provided free-of-charge to an inmate inside a US correctional institution.

Be part of God's Word renewing lives by making a tax-free donation:

Renewing Lives
PO Box **5529**
Diamond Bar, CA 91765-**7529**
www.renewinglives.com

Incarcerated? Please pray for donors to support the printing and mailing of this book. If donations exist for this project, one book will be mailed at no cost to an incarcerated person. Please provide your neatly printed name, ID or Fed A#, birthplace, birthdate, housing/cell, and correctional facility mailing address. *Requests must be written in your own wording, style and handwriting—no form letters, copied/repeated wording, writing as though you are another person, or group/dorm lists with multiple names (but you can mail requests in one envelope to save a stamp).* Requests must be mailed *directly from your institution.* If you have a loved one who is incarcerated they must personally write from their facility. If you do not receive a book within six weeks—our supply was exhausted. We really do need prayer for donors :-)

TABLE OF CONTENTS

Address Book 6

Bible Reading 58

Birthday Tracker 60

Family Records 67

Helpful Info 79

Holidays & Calendars 80

Lists 104

Other LARGE PRINT books available for purchase:

PROVERBIOS en Español, **PROVERBS** in English, Versión Bilingüe—Bilingual Version Letra Grande—18 puntos Reina Valera 1909, Large Print—18 point King James Today

PROVERBS with WORD Journals This book is ideal for personal, student or group Bible study, transitional readers, and the visually impaired. It includes WORD Journal™ pages which encourage you to read the Book of Proverbs on a plan, write a verse you find interesting, pay attention to details you choose to research, then formulate personal application.   With suggestions on how you can use this book, you'll go through a chapter of Proverbs a day, every day or at a do-what-works-for-you pace.
• Large Print 18 point

PROVERBS Writing God's Word Discover the blessing of writing out the word of God, verse-by-verse. This LARGE print workbook will it cause you to slow down, meditate, and memorize as you learn. You'll choose to hand copy the text as it is, write your understanding of it in your own writing style, or pick a Bible version to compare it to. Includes graphics to shade, color, or express creativity. • Large Print 18 point

Read, Write & REAP will keep you *busy in the Bible*™ encouraging spiritual growth, intelligent conversation, and friendly fellowship. The text is formatted so you can read and re-write it line-by-line in your preferred style. At the back of the book you'll find the REAP Bible Study System to: **R**ead the chapter, choose a verse or two hand copy and re-write from a different translation, **E**xamine the text using your favorite resources, **A**cknowledge what God prompts your heart to act upon, attest to personal experiences, then "talk to God" in written **P**rayer. Includes: • Easier–to–read King James Version • Large print 18-20 point • REAP Bible Study System
Titles completed: ❏ Anger in the Bible ❏ Ecclesiastes ❏ John ❏ Philippians

Time in The Word offers a variety of ideas to keep you *busy in the Bible*™ as you read, write, study, and note what you learn in church, at home, or wherever your journey takes you. It includes: •   Bible Art pages to draw your favorite verse •   Blank lines and wide margins for sermon and study notes •   Coloring pages for calm, relaxing, stress relief •   Easier-to-read King James Version • Large Print 18 point

Blessed is he whose transgression is forgiven,

whose sin is covered. Psalm 32:1

5

Name
Address
City, State, Zip
Phone
Email
Notes

Name
Address
City, State, Zip
Phone
Email
Notes

Name
Address
City, State, Zip
Phone
Email
Notes

Name
Address
City, State, Zip
Phone
Email
Notes

Name
Address
City, State, Zip
Phone
Email
Notes

Adam & Eve were expelled from Eden because they

Name _____
Address _____
City, State, Zip _____
Phone _____
Email _____
Notes _____
_____

Name _____
Address _____
City, State, Zip _____
Phone _____
Email _____
Notes _____
_____

Name _____
Address _____
City, State, Zip _____
Phone _____
Email _____
Notes _____
_____

Name _____
Address _____
City, State, Zip _____
Phone _____
Email _____
Notes _____
_____

Name _____
Address _____
City, State, Zip _____
Phone _____
Email _____
Notes _____
_____

B

Name _____
Address _____
City, State, Zip _____
Phone _____
Email _____
Notes _____
_____

Name _____
Address _____
City, State, Zip _____
Phone _____
Email _____
Notes _____
_____

Name _____
Address _____
City, State, Zip _____
Phone _____
Email _____
Notes _____
_____

Name _____
Address _____
City, State, Zip _____
Phone _____
Email _____
Notes _____
_____

Name _____
Address _____
City, State, Zip _____
Phone _____
Email _____
Notes _____
_____

...Turn you unto me, says the LORD of hosts,

Name _____ **B**
Address _____
City, State, Zip _____
Phone _____
Email _____
Notes _____
_____

Name _____
Address _____
City, State, Zip _____
Phone _____
Email _____
Notes _____
_____

Name _____
Address _____
City, State, Zip _____
Phone _____
Email _____
Notes _____
_____

Name _____
Address _____
City, State, Zip _____
Phone _____
Email _____
Notes _____
_____

Name _____
Address _____
City, State, Zip _____
Phone _____
Email _____
Notes _____
_____

Name
Address
City, State, Zip
Phone
Email
Notes

Name
Address
City, State, Zip
Phone
Email
Notes

Name
Address
City, State, Zip
Phone
Email
Notes

Name
Address
City, State, Zip
Phone
Email
Notes

Name
Address
City, State, Zip
Phone
Email
Notes

Delilah cut off Samson's long hair so his strength

Name _____

Address _____

City, State, Zip _____

Phone _____

Email _____

Notes _____

_____

Name _____

Address _____

City, State, Zip _____

Phone _____

Email _____

Notes _____

_____

Name _____

Address _____

City, State, Zip _____

Phone _____

Email _____

Notes _____

_____

Name _____

Address _____

City, State, Zip _____

Phone _____

Email _____

Notes _____

_____

Name _____

Address _____

City, State, Zip _____

Phone _____

Email _____

Notes _____

_____

Name
Address
City, State, Zip
Phone
Email
Notes

Name
Address
City, State, Zip
Phone
Email
Notes

Name
Address
City, State, Zip
Phone
Email
Notes

Name
Address
City, State, Zip
Phone
Email
Notes

Name
Address
City, State, Zip
Phone
Email
Notes

The LORD is good, a strong hold in the day of trouble;

Name _____

Address _____

City, State, Zip _____

Phone _____

Email _____

Notes _____

_____

Name _____

Address _____

City, State, Zip _____

Phone _____

Email _____

Notes _____

_____

Name _____

Address _____

City, State, Zip _____

Phone _____

Email _____

Notes _____

_____

Name _____

Address _____

City, State, Zip _____

Phone _____

Email _____

Notes _____

_____

Name _____

Address _____

City, State, Zip _____

Phone _____

Email _____

Notes _____

_____

and He knows them that trust in Him. Nahum 1:7

Name
Address
City, State, Zip
Phone
Email
Notes

Name
Address
City, State, Zip
Phone
Email
Notes

Name
Address
City, State, Zip
Phone
Email
Notes

Name
Address
City, State, Zip
Phone
Email
Notes

Name
Address
City, State, Zip
Phone
Email
Notes

The word "Rapture" is found in the Bible.

Name _____

Address _____

City, State, Zip _____

Phone _____

Email _____

Notes _____

_____

E

Name _____

Address _____

City, State, Zip _____

Phone _____

Email _____

Notes _____

_____

Name _____

Address _____

City, State, Zip _____

Phone _____

Email _____

Notes _____

_____

Name _____

Address _____

City, State, Zip _____

Phone _____

Email _____

Notes _____

_____

Name _____

Address _____

City, State, Zip _____

Phone _____

Email _____

Notes _____

_____

Name
Address
City, State, Zip
Phone
Email
Notes

Name
Address
City, State, Zip
Phone
Email
Notes

Name
Address
City, State, Zip
Phone
Email
Notes

Name
Address
City, State, Zip
Phone
Email
Notes

Name
Address
City, State, Zip
Phone
Email
Notes

I sought the LORD, and he heard me,

Name
Address
City, State, Zip
Phone
Email
Notes

F

Name
Address
City, State, Zip
Phone
Email
Notes

Name
Address
City, State, Zip
Phone
Email
Notes

Name
Address
City, State, Zip
Phone
Email
Notes

Name
Address
City, State, Zip
Phone
Email
Notes

and delivered me from all my fears. Psalm 34:4

Name
Address
City, State, Zip
Phone
Email
Notes

Name
Address
City, State, Zip
Phone
Email
Notes

Name
Address
City, State, Zip
Phone
Email
Notes

Name
Address
City, State, Zip
Phone
Email
Notes

Name
Address
City, State, Zip
Phone
Email
Notes

Three wise men visited Jesus in a manger.

Name _____
Address _____
City, State, Zip _____
Phone _____
Email _____
Notes _____
_____

Name _____
Address _____
City, State, Zip _____
Phone _____
Email _____
Notes _____
_____

Name _____
Address _____
City, State, Zip _____
Phone _____
Email _____
Notes _____
_____

Name _____
Address _____
City, State, Zip _____
Phone _____
Email _____
Notes _____
_____

Name _____
Address _____
City, State, Zip _____
Phone _____
Email _____
Notes _____
_____

True? or False? Look it up: Matthew 2:11

Name
Address
City, State, Zip
Phone
Email
Notes

Name
Address
City, State, Zip
Phone
Email
Notes

Name
Address
City, State, Zip
Phone
Email
Notes

Name
Address
City, State, Zip
Phone
Email
Notes

Name
Address
City, State, Zip
Phone
Email
Notes

Fret not yourself because of evildoers,

Name
Address
City, State, Zip
Phone
Email
Notes

Name
Address
City, State, Zip
Phone
Email
Notes

H

Name
Address
City, State, Zip
Phone
Email
Notes

Name
Address
City, State, Zip
Phone
Email
Notes

Name
Address
City, State, Zip
Phone
Email
Notes

Name
Address
City, State, Zip
Phone
Email
Notes

Name
Address
City, State, Zip
Phone
Email
Notes

Name
Address
City, State, Zip
Phone
Email
Notes

Name
Address
City, State, Zip
Phone
Email
Notes

Name
Address
City, State, Zip
Phone
Email
Notes

These two verses contain all the letters of the alphabet except one.

Name _____
Address _____
City, State, Zip _____
Phone _____
Email _____
Notes _____
_____

Name _____
Address _____
City, State, Zip _____
Phone _____
Email _____
Notes _____
_____

Name _____
Address _____
City, State, Zip _____
Phone _____
Email _____
Notes _____
_____

Name _____
Address _____
City, State, Zip _____
Phone _____
Email _____
Notes _____
_____

Name _____
Address _____
City, State, Zip _____
Phone _____
Email _____
Notes _____
_____

Name
Address
City, State, Zip
Phone
Email
Notes

Name
Address
City, State, Zip
Phone
Email
Notes

Name
Address
City, State, Zip
Phone
Email
Notes

Name
Address
City, State, Zip
Phone
Email
Notes

Name
Address
City, State, Zip
Phone
Email
Notes

In God have I put my trust:

Name
Address
City, State, Zip
Phone
Email
Notes

Name
Address
City, State, Zip
Phone
Email
Notes

J

Name
Address
City, State, Zip
Phone
Email
Notes

Name
Address
City, State, Zip
Phone
Email
Notes

Name
Address
City, State, Zip
Phone
Email
Notes

Name
Address
City, State, Zip
Phone
Email
Notes

Name
Address
City, State, Zip
Phone
Email
Notes

Name
Address
City, State, Zip
Phone
Email
Notes

Name
Address
City, State, Zip
Phone
Email
Notes

Name
Address
City, State, Zip
Phone
Email
Notes

The word "Eternity" is found in the Bible.

Name _____
Address _____
City, State, Zip _____
Phone _____
Email _____
Notes _____
_____

Name _____
Address _____
City, State, Zip _____
Phone _____
Email _____
Notes _____
_____

Name _____
Address _____
City, State, Zip _____
Phone _____
Email _____
Notes _____
_____

Name _____
Address _____
City, State, Zip _____
Phone _____
Email _____
Notes _____
_____

Name _____
Address _____
City, State, Zip _____
Phone _____
Email _____
Notes _____
_____

True? or False? Look it up: Isaiah 57:15

Name
Address
City, State, Zip
Phone
Email
Notes

Name
Address
City, State, Zip
Phone
Email
Notes

Name
Address
City, State, Zip
Phone
Email
Notes

Name
Address
City, State, Zip
Phone
Email
Notes

Name
Address
City, State, Zip
Phone
Email
Notes

What shall we then say to these things?

Name _____
Address _____
City, State, Zip _____
Phone _____
Email _____
Notes _____
_____

Name _____
Address _____
City, State, Zip _____
Phone _____
Email _____
Notes _____
_____

Name _____
Address _____
City, State, Zip _____
Phone _____
Email _____
Notes _____
_____

Name _____
Address _____
City, State, Zip _____
Phone _____
Email _____
Notes _____
_____

Name _____
Address _____
City, State, Zip _____
Phone _____
Email _____
Notes _____
_____

If God be for us, who can be against us? Romans 8:31

Name
Address
City, State, Zip
Phone
Email
Notes

Name
Address
City, State, Zip
Phone
Email
Notes

 Name
Address
City, State, Zip
Phone
Email
Notes

Name
Address
City, State, Zip
Phone
Email
Notes

Name
Address
City, State, Zip
Phone
Email
Notes

David authored the most writings

Name
Address
City, State, Zip
Phone
Email
Notes

Name
Address
City, State, Zip
Phone
Email
Notes

Name
Address
City, State, Zip
Phone
Email
Notes

Name
Address
City, State, Zip
Phone
Email
Notes

Name
Address
City, State, Zip
Phone
Email
Notes

Name
Address
City, State, Zip
Phone
Email
Notes

Name
Address
City, State, Zip
Phone
Email
Notes

Name
Address
City, State, Zip
Phone
Email
Notes

Name
Address
City, State, Zip
Phone
Email
Notes

Name
Address
City, State, Zip
Phone
Email
Notes

And whatsoever you do, do it heartily,

Name _____
Address _____
City, State, Zip _____
Phone _____
Email _____
Notes _____
_____

Name _____
Address _____
City, State, Zip _____
Phone _____
Email _____
Notes _____
_____

Name _____
Address _____
City, State, Zip _____
Phone _____
Email _____
Notes _____
_____

Name _____
Address _____
City, State, Zip _____
Phone _____
Email _____
Notes _____
_____

Name _____
Address _____
City, State, Zip _____
Phone _____
Email _____
Notes _____
_____

Name
Address
City, State, Zip
Phone
Email
Notes

Name
Address
City, State, Zip
Phone
Email
Notes

Name
Address
City, State, Zip
Phone
Email
Notes

Name
Address
City, State, Zip
Phone
Email
Notes

Name
Address
City, State, Zip
Phone
Email
Notes

The first book to ever be printed

Name _____
Address _____
City, State, Zip _____
Phone _____
Email _____
Notes _____
_____

Name _____
Address _____
City, State, Zip _____
Phone _____
Email _____
Notes _____
_____

Name _____
Address _____
City, State, Zip _____
Phone _____
Email _____
Notes _____
_____

Name _____
Address _____
City, State, Zip _____
Phone _____
Email _____
Notes _____
_____

Name _____
Address _____
City, State, Zip _____
Phone _____
Email _____
Notes _____
_____

in all history is the Bible. True? or False?

Name
Address
City, State, Zip
Phone
Email
Notes

Name
Address
City, State, Zip
Phone
Email
Notes

Name
Address
City, State, Zip
Phone
Email
Notes

Name
Address
City, State, Zip
Phone
Email
Notes

Name
Address
City, State, Zip
Phone
Email
Notes

For what shall it profit a man, if he shall gain the whole world,

Name
Address
City, State, Zip
Phone
Email
Notes

Name
Address
City, State, Zip
Phone
Email
Notes

Name
Address
City, State, Zip
Phone
Email
Notes

P

Name
Address
City, State, Zip
Phone
Email
Notes

Name
Address
City, State, Zip
Phone
Email
Notes

and lose his own soul? Mark 8:36-37

Name
Address
City, State, Zip
Phone
Email
Notes

Name
Address
City, State, Zip
Phone
Email
Notes

Name
Address
City, State, Zip
Phone
Email
Notes

Name
Address
City, State, Zip
Phone
Email
Notes

Name
Address
City, State, Zip
Phone
Email
Notes

Two books in the Bible do not mention the word "God".

Name _____
Address _____
City, State, Zip _____
Phone _____
Email _____
Notes _____
_____

Name _____
Address _____
City, State, Zip _____
Phone _____
Email _____
Notes _____
_____

Name _____
Address _____
City, State, Zip _____
Phone _____
Email _____
Notes _____
_____

Name _____
Address _____
City, State, Zip _____
Phone _____
Email _____
Notes _____
_____

Name _____
Address _____
City, State, Zip _____
Phone _____
Email _____
Notes _____
_____

True? or False? Look it up: Esther, Song of Solomon

Name
Address
City, State, Zip
Phone
Email
Notes

Name
Address
City, State, Zip
Phone
Email
Notes

Name
Address
City, State, Zip
Phone
Email
Notes

 Name
Address
City, State, Zip
Phone
Email
Notes

Name
Address
City, State, Zip
Phone
Email
Notes

Submit yourselves therefore to God.

Name
Address
City, State, Zip
Phone
Email
Notes

Name
Address
City, State, Zip
Phone
Email
Notes

Name
Address
City, State, Zip
Phone
Email
Notes

Name
Address
City, State, Zip
Phone
Email
Notes

R

Name
Address
City, State, Zip
Phone
Email
Notes

Resist the devil, and he will flee from you. James 4:7

Name
Address
City, State, Zip
Phone
Email
Notes

Name
Address
City, State, Zip
Phone
Email
Notes

Name
Address
City, State, Zip
Phone
Email
Notes

Name
Address
City, State, Zip
Phone
Email
Notes

Name
Address
City, State, Zip
Phone
Email
Notes

Two men of Old Testament times did not die.

Name _____

Address _____

City, State, Zip _____

Phone _____

Email _____

Notes _____

_____

Name _____

Address _____

City, State, Zip _____

Phone _____

Email _____

Notes _____

_____

Name _____

Address _____

City, State, Zip _____

Phone _____

Email _____

Notes _____

_____

Name _____

Address _____

City, State, Zip _____

Phone _____

Email _____

Notes _____

_____

Name _____

Address _____

City, State, Zip _____

Phone _____

Email _____

Notes _____

_____

Name
Address
City, State, Zip
Phone
Email
Notes

Name
Address
City, State, Zip
Phone
Email
Notes

Name
Address
City, State, Zip
Phone
Email
Notes

Name
Address
City, State, Zip
Phone
Email
Notes

Name
Address
City, State, Zip
Phone
Email
Notes

But seek ye first the kingdom of God, and his righteousness;

Name _____

Address _____

City, State, Zip _____

Phone _____

Email _____

Notes _____

_____

Name _____

Address _____

City, State, Zip _____

Phone _____

Email _____

Notes _____

_____

Name _____

Address _____

City, State, Zip _____

Phone _____

Email _____

Notes _____

_____

Name _____

Address _____

City, State, Zip _____

Phone _____

Email _____

Notes _____

_____

Name _____

Address _____

City, State, Zip _____

Phone _____

Email _____

Notes _____

_____

and all these things shall be added unto you. Matthew 6:33

Name
Address
City, State, Zip
Phone
Email
Notes

Name
Address
City, State, Zip
Phone
Email
Notes

Name
Address
City, State, Zip
Phone
Email
Notes

Name
Address
City, State, Zip
Phone
Email
Notes

Name
Address
City, State, Zip
Phone
Email
Notes

More Bibles have been purchased and shoplifted

Name _____

Address _____

City, State, Zip _____

Phone _____

Email _____

Notes _____

_____

Name _____

Address _____

City, State, Zip _____

Phone _____

Email _____

Notes _____

_____

Name _____

Address _____

City, State, Zip _____

Phone _____

Email _____

Notes _____

_____

Name _____

Address _____

City, State, Zip _____

Phone _____

Email _____

Notes _____

_____

U

Name _____

Address _____

City, State, Zip _____

Phone _____

Email _____

Notes _____

_____

than any other book in all of history. True? or False?

Name
Address
City, State, Zip
Phone
Email
Notes

Name
Address
City, State, Zip
Phone
Email
Notes

Name
Address
City, State, Zip
Phone
Email
Notes

Name
Address
City, State, Zip
Phone
Email
Notes

Name
Address
City, State, Zip
Phone
Email
Notes

The King James Bible has inspired the lyrics of

Name
Address
City, State, Zip
Phone
Email
Notes

Name
Address
City, State, Zip
Phone
Email
Notes

Name
Address
City, State, Zip
Phone
Email
Notes

Name
Address
City, State, Zip
Phone
Email
Notes

Name
Address
City, State, Zip
Phone
Email
Notes

more pop songs than any other book. True? or False?

Name
Address
City, State, Zip
Phone
Email
Notes

Name
Address
City, State, Zip
Phone
Email
Notes

Name
Address
City, State, Zip
Phone
Email
Notes

Name
Address
City, State, Zip
Phone
Email
Notes

Name
Address
City, State, Zip
Phone
Email
Notes

Can you describe the days of creation in order? Genesis 1:1–2:3

Name
Address
City, State, Zip
Phone
Email
Notes

Name
Address
City, State, Zip
Phone
Email
Notes

Name
Address
City, State, Zip
Phone
Email
Notes

Name
Address
City, State, Zip
Phone
Email
Notes

Name
Address
City, State, Zip
Phone
Email
Notes

Name
Address
City, State, Zip
Phone
Email
Notes

Name
Address
City, State, Zip
Phone
Email
Notes

Name
Address
City, State, Zip
Phone
Email
Notes

Name
Address
City, State, Zip
Phone
Email
Notes

Name
Address
City, State, Zip
Phone
Email
Notes

Be sober, be vigilant; because your adversary the devil, as a

Name _____
Address _____
City, State, Zip _____
Phone _____
Email _____
Notes _____
_____

Name _____
Address _____
City, State, Zip _____
Phone _____
Email _____
Notes _____
_____

Name _____
Address _____
City, State, Zip _____
Phone _____
Email _____
Notes _____
_____

Name _____
Address _____
City, State, Zip _____
Phone _____
Email _____
Notes _____
_____

Name _____
Address _____
City, State, Zip _____
Phone _____
Email _____
Notes _____
_____

roaring lion, walks about, seeking whom he may devour: 1 Peter 5:8

Name
Address
City, State, Zip
Phone
Email
Notes

Name
Address
City, State, Zip
Phone
Email
Notes

Name
Address
City, State, Zip
Phone
Email
Notes

Name
Address
City, State, Zip
Phone
Email
Notes

Name
Address
City, State, Zip
Phone
Email
Notes

But the LORD your God you shall fear; and He shall deliver you

Name
Address
City, State, Zip
Phone
Email
Notes

Name
Address
City, State, Zip
Phone
Email
Notes

Name
Address
City, State, Zip
Phone
Email
Notes

Name
Address
City, State, Zip
Phone
Email
Notes

Name
Address
City, State, Zip
Phone
Email
Notes

out of the hand of all your enemies. 2 Kings 17:39

Name
Address
City, State, Zip
Phone
Email
Notes

Name
Address
City, State, Zip
Phone
Email
Notes

Name
Address
City, State, Zip
Phone
Email
Notes

Name
Address
City, State, Zip
Phone
Email
Notes

Name
Address
City, State, Zip
Phone
Email
Notes

Z

Wait on the LORD: be of good courage, and

Name
Address
City, State, Zip
Phone
Email
Notes

Name
Address
City, State, Zip
Phone
Email
Notes

Name
Address
City, State, Zip
Phone
Email
Notes

Name
Address
City, State, Zip
Phone
Email
Notes

Name
Address
City, State, Zip
Phone
Email
Notes

He shall strengthen your heart: wait, I say, on the LORD.   Psalm 27:14   **Z 57**

Bible Reading Plan Ideas:

Read the Bible in a Year

Believe it or not, you only have to read a little over three chapters of the Bible a day to finish the whole book within a year. There are 1189 chapters in the Bible, which divided by 365 days equals 3.26 chapters a day. Or, try three chapters a day and five on Sundays. *You can do it!*

Got 70 hours?

The Bible can be read cover-to-cover in about seventy hours. Seven boxes are provided to track the number of times you've finished a plan.

❏ 1 ❏ 2 ❏ 3 ❏ 4 ❏ 5 ❏ 6 ❏ 7

Read the Bible in a Little Over Three Years

If you slow down and concentrate on reading just one chapter of the Bible every single day, you will finish with greater insight—in a little over three years! *You'll get to know God's word better!*

❏ Old Testament   ❏ 1 ❏ 2 ❏ 3 ❏ 4 ❏ 5 ❏ 6 ❏ 7

❏ New Testament   ❏ 1 ❏ 2 ❏ 3 ❏ 4 ❏ 5 ❏ 6 ❏ 7

❏ Entire Bible   ❏ 1 ❏ 2 ❏ 3 ❏ 4 ❏ 5 ❏ 6 ❏ 7

For days when your normal schedule is disrupted try this:

Look at a calendar and base your reading on today's date—for instance, if today is the first (1st) read:

Genesis 1 and/or   John 1
Psalm 1 and/or   Proverbs 1

Then on the second (2nd) read:

Genesis 2 and/or   John 2
Psalm 2 and/or   Proverbs 2

❏ Book of Genesis ❏ 1 ❏ 2 ❏ 3 ❏ 4 ❏ 5 ❏ 6 ❏ 7

❏ Book of John ❏ 1 ❏ 2 ❏ 3 ❏ 4 ❏ 5 ❏ 6 ❏ 7

❏ Book of Psalms ❏ 1 ❏ 2 ❏ 3 ❏ 4 ❏ 5 ❏ 6 ❏ 7

❏ Book of Proverbs ❏ 1 ❏ 2 ❏ 3 ❏ 4 ❏ 5 ❏ 6 ❏ 7

If you like this plan, change it up next month—pick different books.

For there is one God, and one mediator between God and men, the

FEBRUARY

1 ☐ _____	
2 ☐ _____	
3 ☐ _____	
4 ☐ _____	
5 ☐ _____	
6 ☐ _____	
7 ☐ _____	
8 ☐ _____	
9 ☐ _____	
10 ☐ _____	

_____
_____
_____
4 ☐ _____
5 ☐ _____
6 ☐ _____
7 ☐ _____
8 ☐ _____
9 ☐ _____
10 ☐ _____
11 ☐ _____
12 ☐ _____
13 ☐ _____
14 ☐ _____
15 ☐ _____
16 ☐ _____
17 ☐ _____
18 ☐ _____
19 ☐ _____
20 ☐ _____
21 ☐ _____
22 ☐ _____
23 ☐ _____
24 ☐ _____
25 ☐ _____
26 ☐ _____
27 ☐ _____
28 ☐ _____
29 ☐ _____
30 ☐ _____
31 ☐ _____

FEBRUARY column:
1 ☐ _____
2 ☐ _____
3 ☐ _____
4 ☐ _____
5 ☐ _____
6 ☐ _____
7 ☐ _____
8 ☐ _____
9 ☐ _____
10 ☐ _____
11 ☐ _____
12 ☐ _____
13 ☐ _____
14 ☐ _____
15 ☐ _____
16 ☐ _____
17 ☐ _____
18 ☐ _____
19 ☐ _____
20 ☐ _____
21 ☐ _____
22 ☐ _____
23 ☐ _____
24 ☐ _____
25 ☐ _____
26 ☐ _____
27 ☐ _____
28 ☐ _____
29 ☐ _____

**Record loved ones birthdays
on their date line.**

The last word in the Bible is "Amen".

MARCH

1 ☐ _____
2 ☐ _____
3 ☐ _____
4 ☐ _____
5 ☐ _____
6 ☐ _____
7 ☐ _____
8 ☐ _____
9 ☐ _____
10 ☐ _____
11 ☐ _____
12 ☐ _____
13 ☐ _____
14 ☐ _____
15 ☐ _____
16 ☐ _____
17 ☐ _____
18 ☐ _____
19 ☐ _____
20 ☐ _____
21 ☐ _____
22 ☐ _____
23 ☐ _____
24 ☐ _____
25 ☐ _____
26 ☐ _____
27 ☐ _____
28 ☐ _____
29 ☐ _____
30 ☐ _____
31 ☐ _____

APRIL

1 ☐ _____
2 ☐ _____
3 ☐ _____
4 ☐ _____
5 ☐ _____
6 ☐ _____
7 ☐ _____
8 ☐ _____
9 ☐ _____
10 ☐ _____
11 ☐ _____
12 ☐ _____
13 ☐ _____
14 ☐ _____
15 ☐ _____
16 ☐ _____
17 ☐ _____
18 ☐ _____
19 ☐ _____
20 ☐ _____
21 ☐ _____
22 ☐ _____
23 ☐ _____
24 ☐ _____
25 ☐ _____
26 ☐ _____
27 ☐ _____
28 ☐ _____
29 ☐ _____
30 ☐ _____

True? or False? Look it up: Revelation 22:   **61**

MAY

1 ☐ _____
2 ☐ _____
3 ☐ _____
4 ☐ _____
5 ☐ _____
6 ☐ _____
7 ☐ _____
8 ☐ _____
9 ☐ _____
10 ☐ _____
11 ☐ _____
12 ☐ _____
13 ☐ _____
14 ☐ _____
15 ☐ _____
16 ☐ _____
17 ☐ _____
18 ☐ _____
19 ☐ _____
20 ☐ _____
21 ☐ _____
22 ☐ _____
23 ☐ _____
24 ☐ _____
25 ☐ _____
26 ☐ _____
27 ☐ _____
28 ☐ _____
29 ☐ _____
30 ☐ _____
31 ☐ _____

JUNE

1 ☐ _____
2 ☐ _____
3 ☐ _____
4 ☐ _____
5 ☐ _____
6 ☐ _____
7 ☐ _____
8 ☐ _____
9 ☐ _____
10 ☐ _____
11 ☐ _____
12 ☐ _____
13 ☐ _____
14 ☐ _____
15 ☐ _____
16 ☐ _____
17 ☐ _____
18 ☐ _____
19 ☐ _____
20 ☐ _____
21 ☐ _____
22 ☐ _____
23 ☐ _____
24 ☐ _____
25 ☐ _____
26 ☐ _____
27 ☐ _____
28 ☐ _____
29 ☐ _____
30 ☐ _____

**Record loved ones birthdays
on their date line.**

But he gives more grace. Wherefore he said,

JULY

1 ☐ _____
2 ☐ _____
3 ☐ _____
4 ☐ _____
5 ☐ _____
6 ☐ _____
7 ☐ _____
8 ☐ _____
9 ☐ _____
10 ☐ _____
11 ☐ _____
12 ☐ _____
13 ☐ _____
14 ☐ _____
15 ☐ _____
16 ☐ _____
17 ☐ _____
18 ☐ _____
19 ☐ _____
20 ☐ _____
21 ☐ _____
22 ☐ _____
23 ☐ _____
24 ☐ _____
25 ☐ _____
26 ☐ _____
27 ☐ _____
28 ☐ _____
29 ☐ _____
30 ☐ _____
31 ☐ _____

AUGUST

1 ☐ _____
2 ☐ _____
3 ☐ _____
4 ☐ _____
5 ☐ _____
6 ☐ _____
7 ☐ _____
8 ☐ _____
9 ☐ _____
10 ☐ _____
11 ☐ _____
12 ☐ _____
13 ☐ _____
14 ☐ _____
15 ☐ _____
16 ☐ _____
17 ☐ _____
18 ☐ _____
19 ☐ _____
20 ☐ _____
21 ☐ _____
22 ☐ _____
23 ☐ _____
24 ☐ _____
25 ☐ _____
26 ☐ _____
27 ☐ _____
28 ☐ _____
29 ☐ _____
30 ☐ _____
31 ☐ _____

God resists the proud, but gives grace unto the humble. James 4:6

SEPTEMBER

1 ❑ _____
2 ❑ _____
3 ❑ _____
4 ❑ _____
5 ❑ _____
6 ❑ _____
7 ❑ _____
8 ❑ _____
9 ❑ _____
10 ❑ _____
11 ❑ _____
12 ❑ _____
13 ❑ _____
14 ❑ _____
15 ❑ _____
16 ❑ _____
17 ❑ _____
18 ❑ _____
19 ❑ _____
20 ❑ _____
21 ❑ _____
22 ❑ _____
23 ❑ _____
24 ❑ _____
25 ❑ _____
26 ❑ _____
27 ❑ _____
28 ❑ _____
29 ❑ _____
30 ❑ _____

**Record loved ones birthdays
on their date line.**

OCTOBER

1 ❑ _____
2 ❑ _____
3 ❑ _____
4 ❑ _____
5 ❑ _____
6 ❑ _____
7 ❑ _____
8 ❑ _____
9 ❑ _____
10 ❑ _____
11 ❑ _____
12 ❑ _____
13 ❑ _____
14 ❑ _____
15 ❑ _____
16 ❑ _____
17 ❑ _____
18 ❑ _____
19 ❑ _____
20 ❑ _____
21 ❑ _____
22 ❑ _____
23 ❑ _____
24 ❑ _____
25 ❑ _____
26 ❑ _____
27 ❑ _____
28 ❑ _____
29 ❑ _____
30 ❑ _____
31 ❑ _____

If we confess our sins, he is faithful and just to forgive us our sins,

NOVEMBER

1 ❏ _____
2 ❏ _____
3 ❏ _____
4 ❏ _____
5 ❏ _____
6 ❏ _____
7 ❏ _____
8 ❏ _____
9 ❏ _____
10 ❏ _____
11 ❏ _____
12 ❏ _____
13 ❏ _____
14 ❏ _____
15 ❏ _____
16 ❏ _____
17 ❏ _____
18 ❏ _____
19 ❏ _____
20 ❏ _____
21 ❏ _____
22 ❏ _____
23 ❏ _____
24 ❏ _____
25 ❏ _____
26 ❏ _____
27 ❏ _____
28 ❏ _____
29 ❏ _____
30 ❏ _____

DECEMBER

1 ❏ _____
2 ❏ _____
3 ❏ _____
4 ❏ _____
5 ❏ _____
6 ❏ _____
7 ❏ _____
8 ❏ _____
9 ❏ _____
10 ❏ _____
11 ❏ _____
12 ❏ _____
13 ❏ _____
14 ❏ _____
15 ❏ _____
16 ❏ _____
17 ❏ _____
18 ❏ _____
19 ❏ _____
20 ❏ _____
21 ❏ _____
22 ❏ _____
23 ❏ _____
24 ❏ _____
25 ❏ _____
26 ❏ _____
27 ❏ _____
28 ❏ _____
29 ❏ _____
30 ❏ _____
31 ❏ _____

and to cleanse us from all unrighteousness. 1 John 1:9

MY CHARACTER STRENGTHS & PERSONAL VIRTUES

1 _____
2 _____
3 _____
4 _____
5 _____
6 _____
7 _____
8 _____
9 _____
10 _____
11 _____
12 _____
13 _____
14 _____
15 _____
16 _____
17 _____
18 _____
19 _____
20 _____
21 _____
22 _____
23 _____
24 _____
25 _____
26 _____
27 _____
28 _____
29 _____
30 _____
31 _____
32 _____
33 _____
34 _____
35 _____

36 _____
37 _____
38 _____
39 _____
40 _____
41 _____
42 _____
43 _____
44 _____
45 _____
46 _____
47 _____
48 _____
49 _____
50 _____
51 _____
52 _____
53 _____
54 _____
55 _____
56 _____
57 _____
58 _____
59 _____
60 _____
61 _____
62 _____
63 _____
64 _____
65 _____
66 _____
67 _____
68 _____
69 _____
70 _____

An apple tree is mentioned in the Book

ME

First _____

Middle _____

Last NAME _____

Address _____

_____

City/State/Zip _____

Email _____

Phone _____   Phone _____

ICE In Case of Emergency

Name _____
Address _____
City/State/Zip _____
Relationship _____
Phone _____   Phone _____
Email _____

Name _____
Address _____
City/State/Zip _____
Relationship _____
Phone _____   Phone _____
Email _____

Name _____
Address _____
City/State/Zip _____
Relationship _____
Phone _____   Phone _____
Email _____

of Genesis. True? or False?

MY WORK & MEASUREMENTS

MY WORK

Employer _____

Supervisor _____

My Job Title _____

Address _____

City/State/Zip _____

Phone _____

Fax_____

Work Email _____

Website URL *www.* _____

Employer _____

Supervisor _____

My Job Title _____

Address _____

City/State/Zip _____

Phone _____

Fax_____

Work Email _____

Website URL *www.* _____

MY MEASUREMENTS SHOPPING GUIDE

Bicep L_____	Bicep R _____	Bust Upper ____	Bust _____	Bust Lower ____
Calf L _____	Calf R_____	Chest _____	Head _____	Hips_____
Inseam_____	Neck _____	Outseam_____	Ring _____	Shoulder _____
Sleeve _____	Thigh L_____	Thigh R_____	Waist _____	Waist Low ____

Blouse _____	Dress_____	Hat _____	Jacket_____	Levis _____
Pant _____	Shirt_____	Shorts _____	Skirt _____	Slip _____
Suit _____	Sweater _____	Swim Suit ____	T Shirt _____	Other _____

Philistines mistreated the Ark of the Covenant and were plagued by painful

 # MY EDUCATION & SERVICE

Grade School(s) & Year(s) _____

_____

_____

Middle/Jr. High School/Year(s) _____

_____

_____

High/Cont./GED School/Year(s) _____

_____

_____

Religious Studies/Year(s) _____

_____

_____

College & Degree/Year(s) _____

_____

_____

Graduate School, Degree(s), Year(s) _____

_____

_____

Trade/Vocational School/Year(s) _____

_____

_____

Military Service/Year(s) _____

_____

_____

Certificates/Training _____

_____

_____

Volunteer Service/Work _____

_____

_____

hemorrhoids (emerods). True or False?   Look it up: 1 Samuel 5   **69**

MORE ON ME

Birthdate _____

Birthplace_____

Religion/Spirituality/Belief's _____

_____

Place of meeting or worship_____

Religious/Spiritual leader that might know me best _____

Address _____

❏ Single ❏ Engaged ❏ Married ❏ Widowed ❏ Divorced

Maiden Name (or **A**lso **K**nown **A**s): _____

_____

Spouse's Name (or **A**lso **K**nown **A**s): _____

_____

❏ I have a library card. ❏ I have a current/valid passport.

❏ I have DMV issued REAL driver's license or ❏ REAL identification card.

❏ I have an original certificate of Baptism.

❏ I have an original or a certified copy of my birth certificate.

❏ I have an original or a certified copy of my marriage certificate.

❏ I have an original or a certified copy of the final decree of divorce.

❏ I have an easily accessible government issued original social security card.

❏ I have an original or a certified copy of each of my children's birth certificates.

❏ I have an original or a certified copy of my deceased spouse's death certificate.

❏ I am currently incarcerated and have written for reentry information:

    Root & Rebound, 1730 Franklin Street, Suite 300, Oakland, CA 94612 for:

    ❏ Confidential, **legal mail** questions

    Free "know-your-rights" **toolkits** ❏ Reentry Planning ❏ my education, my freedom

    ❏ Reentry Advocacy Center **legal hotline** Mon–Fri 9:00a–5:00p (510) 279-4662

      (accepts collect calls from the incarcerated)

MY HEALTH

Height _____ Blood Type_____

Date	Weight	BMI	Date	Weight	BMI	Date	Weight	BMI

Allergies_____

_____

_____

HDL Cholesterol	LD	TRI	Total

Surgeries _____

_____

_____

_____

❏ I have a notarized Advance Healthcare Directive—so my wishes are followed.
❏ I have a notarized Healthcare Power of Attorney—to put my loved one in charge.

Date	Blood Pressure	Date	Blood Pressure	Date	Blood Pressure

MY CHILDREN

1 _____ Birthdate _____
❏ Adopted ❏ Biological ❏ Step ❏ Deceased _____ Cause _____

2 _____ Birthdate _____
❏ Adopted ❏ Biological ❏ Step ❏ Deceased _____ Cause _____

3 _____ Birthdate _____
❏ Adopted ❏ Biological ❏ Step ❏ Deceased _____ Cause _____

4 _____ Birthdate _____
❏ Adopted ❏ Biological ❏ Step ❏ Deceased _____ Cause _____

5 _____ Birthdate _____
❏ Adopted ❏ Biological ❏ Step ❏ Deceased _____ Cause _____

6 _____ Birthdate _____
❏ Adopted ❏ Biological ❏ Step ❏ Deceased _____ Cause _____

7 _____ Birthdate _____
❏ Adopted ❏ Biological ❏ Step ❏ Deceased _____ Cause _____

8 _____ Birthdate _____
❏ Adopted ❏ Biological ❏ Step ❏ Deceased _____ Cause _____

9 _____ Birthdate _____
❏ Adopted ❏ Biological ❏ Step ❏ Deceased _____ Cause _____

10 _____ Birthdate _____
❏ Adopted ❏ Biological ❏ Step ❏ Deceased _____ Cause _____

11 _____ Birthdate _____
❏ Adopted ❏ Biological ❏ Step ❏ Deceased _____ Cause _____

12 _____ Birthdate _____
❏ Adopted ❏ Biological ❏ Step ❏ Deceased _____ Cause _____

13 _____ Birthdate _____
❏ Adopted ❏ Biological ❏ Step ❏ Deceased _____ Cause _____

For the LORD knows the way of the righteous:

FAMILY MARRIAGES

Between: _____
Wedding Date _____ Location _____
Date Divorced _____ Deceased _____ Cause _____

Between: _____
Wedding Date _____ Location _____
Date Divorced _____ Deceased _____ Cause _____

Between: _____
Wedding Date _____ Location _____
Date Divorced _____ Deceased _____ Cause _____

Between: _____
Wedding Date _____ Location _____
Date Divorced _____ Deceased _____ Cause _____

Between: _____
Wedding Date _____ Location _____
Date Divorced _____ Deceased _____ Cause _____

Between: _____
Wedding Date _____ Location _____
Date Divorced _____ Deceased _____ Cause _____

Between: _____
Wedding Date _____ Location _____
Date Divorced _____ Deceased _____ Cause _____

Between: _____
Wedding Date _____ Location _____
Date Divorced _____ Deceased _____ Cause _____

but the way of the ungodly shall perish. Psalm 1:6

MY FAMILY TREE

MATERNAL

My Mother _____
❑ Adopted ❑ Biological ❑ Step ❑ Deceased Date _____ Cause _____

My Mother _____
❑ Adopted ❑ Biological ❑ Step ❑ Deceased Date _____ Cause _____

Grandmother (Mom's mom) _____
❑ Adopted ❑ Biological ❑ Step ❑ Deceased Date _____ Cause _____

Grandfather (Mom's dad) _____
❑ Adopted ❑ Biological ❑ Step ❑ Deceased Date _____ Cause _____

Great Grandmother (Grandmother's mom) _____
❑ Adopted ❑ Biological ❑ Step ❑ Deceased Date _____ Cause _____

Great Grandfather (Grandmother's dad) _____
❑ Adopted ❑ Biological ❑ Step ❑ Deceased Date _____ Cause _____

MATERNAL RELATIVES

Mother's Brothers (My Uncles), Spouses (Aunts by marriage) & children (My cousins)

_____ | _____
_____ | _____
_____ | _____
_____ | _____
_____ | _____

Mother's Sisters (My Aunts), Spouses (Uncles by marriage) & children (My cousins)

_____ | _____
_____ | _____
_____ | _____
_____ | _____
_____ | _____

Noah shut the door of the Ark.

MY FAMILY TREE

PATERNAL

My Father_____

❑ Adopted ❑ Biological ❑ Step ❑ Deceased Date _____ Cause _____

My Father_____

❑ Adopted ❑ Biological ❑ Step ❑ Deceased Date _____ Cause _____

Grandmother (Dad's mom)_____

❑ Adopted ❑ Biological ❑ Step ❑ Deceased Date _____ Cause _____

Grandfather (Dad's dad) _____

❑ Adopted ❑ Biological ❑ Step ❑ Deceased Date _____ Cause _____

Great Grandmother (Grandfather's mom) _____

❑ Adopted ❑ Biological ❑ Step ❑ Deceased Date _____ Cause _____

Great Grandfather (Grandfather's dad) _____

❑ Adopted ❑ Biological ❑ Step ❑ Deceased Date _____ Cause _____

PATERNAL RELATIVES

Father's Brothers (My Uncles), Spouses (Aunts by marriage) & children (My cousins)

_____ | _____
_____ | _____
_____ | _____
_____ | _____
_____ | _____

Father's Sisters (My Aunts), Spouses (Uncles by marriage) & children (My cousins)

_____ | _____
_____ | _____
_____ | _____
_____ | _____
_____ | _____

True? or False? Look it up: Genesis 7

MY GRANDCHILDREN & GREAT GRANDCHILDREN

1 _____ Birthdate _____
 ❏ Adopted ❏ Biological ❏ Step ❏ Deceased _____ Cause _____

2 _____ Birthdate _____
 ❏ Adopted ❏ Biological ❏ Step ❏ Deceased _____ Cause _____

3 _____ Birthdate _____
 ❏ Adopted ❏ Biological ❏ Step ❏ Deceased _____ Cause _____

4 _____ Birthdate _____
 ❏ Adopted ❏ Biological ❏ Step ❏ Deceased _____ Cause _____

5 _____ Birthdate _____
 ❏ Adopted ❏ Biological ❏ Step ❏ Deceased _____ Cause _____

6 _____ Birthdate _____
 ❏ Adopted ❏ Biological ❏ Step ❏ Deceased _____ Cause _____

7 _____ Birthdate _____
 ❏ Adopted ❏ Biological ❏ Step ❏ Deceased _____ Cause _____

8 _____ Birthdate _____
 ❏ Adopted ❏ Biological ❏ Step ❏ Deceased _____ Cause _____

9 _____ Birthdate _____
 ❏ Adopted ❏ Biological ❏ Step ❏ Deceased _____ Cause _____

10 _____ Birthdate _____
 ❏ Adopted ❏ Biological ❏ Step ❏ Deceased _____ Cause _____

11 _____ Birthdate _____
 ❏ Adopted ❏ Biological ❏ Step ❏ Deceased _____ Cause _____

12 _____ Birthdate _____
 ❏ Adopted ❏ Biological ❏ Step ❏ Deceased _____ Cause _____

13 _____ Birthdate _____
 ❏ Adopted ❏ Biological ❏ Step ❏ Deceased _____ Cause _____

Be not wise in your own eyes:

MY GRANDCHILDREN & GREAT GRANDCHILDREN

14 _____ Birthdate _____
❏ Adopted ❏ Biological ❏ Step ❏ Deceased_____ Cause _____

15 _____ Birthdate _____
❏ Adopted ❏ Biological ❏ Step ❏ Deceased_____ Cause _____

16 _____ Birthdate _____
❏ Adopted ❏ Biological ❏ Step ❏ Deceased_____ Cause _____

17 _____ Birthdate _____
❏ Adopted ❏ Biological ❏ Step ❏ Deceased_____ Cause _____

18 _____ Birthdate _____
❏ Adopted ❏ Biological ❏ Step ❏ Deceased_____ Cause _____

19 _____ Birthdate _____
❏ Adopted ❏ Biological ❏ Step ❏ Deceased_____ Cause _____

20 _____ Birthdate _____
❏ Adopted ❏ Biological ❏ Step ❏ Deceased_____ Cause _____

21 _____ Birthdate _____
❏ Adopted ❏ Biological ❏ Step ❏ Deceased_____ Cause _____

22 _____ Birthdate _____
❏ Adopted ❏ Biological ❏ Step ❏ Deceased_____ Cause _____

23 _____ Birthdate _____
❏ Adopted ❏ Biological ❏ Step ❏ Deceased_____ Cause _____

24 _____ Birthdate _____
❏ Adopted ❏ Biological ❏ Step ❏ Deceased_____ Cause _____

25 _____ Birthdate _____
❏ Adopted ❏ Biological ❏ Step ❏ Deceased_____ Cause _____

26 _____ Birthdate _____
❏ Adopted ❏ Biological ❏ Step ❏ Deceased_____ Cause _____

fear the LORD, and depart from evil. Proverbs 3:7

MY LOVED-ONE'S HEALTH

Injuries, Illnesses, Hospitalization & Surgeries

Date Family Member   Health Issue(s)

Repent, and turn yourselves from all your transgressions;

US Territories

AL	Alabama
AK	Alaska
AZ	Arizona
AR	Arkansas
CA	California
CO	Colorado
CT	Connecticut
DE	Delaware
DC	District of Columbia
FL	Florida
GA	Georgia
HI	Hawaii
ID	Idaho
IL	Illinois
IN	Indiana
IA	Iowa
KS	Kansas
KY	Kentucky
LA	Louisiana
ME	Maine
MD	Maryland
MA	Massachusetts
MI	Michigan
MN	Minnesota
MS	Mississippi
MO	Missouri
MT	Montana
NE	Nebraska
NV	Nevada
NH	New Hampshire
NJ	New Jersey
NM	New Mexico
NY	New York
NC	North Carolina
ND	North Dakota
OH	Ohio
OK	Oklahoma
OR	Oregon
PA	Pennsylvania
RI	Rhode Island
SC	South Carolina
SD	South Dakota
TN	Tennessee
TX	Texas
UT	Utah
VT	Vermont
VA	Virginia
WA	Washington
WV	West Virginia
WI	Wisconsin
WY	Wyoming
PR	Puerto Rico
VI	Virgin Islands
AS	American Samoa
GU	Guam
MP	N Mariana Islands

Roman / Arabic

Roman	Arabic
I	1
II	2
III	3
IV	4
V	5
VI	6
VII	7
VIII	8
IX	9
X	10
L	50
C	100
D	500
CMXCIX	999
M	1000

USPS Letter
3.5 oz or less
(about 1 Env & 2 Pages)
Min 5"w, max 11.5"w
Min 3.5"h, max 6.125"h
Add $.20 if square

USPS Postcard
Min 5"w, max 6"w
Min 3.5"h, max 4.25"h
Must be rectangular
No folds

Temp

°C	°F
0	32
5	41
10	50
15	59
20	68
25	77
30	86
35	95
40	104
45	113
50	122

Military Time 24 Hour Clock

0100	1:00 A	1300	1:00 P
0200	2:00 A	1400	2:00 P
0300	3:00 A	1500	3:00 P
0400	4:00 A	1600	4:00 P
0500	5:00 A	1700	5:00 P
0600	6:00 A	1800	6:00 P
0700	7:00 A	1900	7:00 P
0800	8:00 A	2000	8:00 P
0900	9:00 A	2100	9:00 P
1000	10:00 A	2200	10:00 P
1100	11:00 A	2300	11:00 P
1200	12:00 P	2400	12:00 A

Weights & Measurements
4 tablespoons = 1/4 cup
1/4 cup = 2 ounces
1 cup = 8 ounces (oz) or 240 milliliters
1 pint = 2 cups (16 oz)
2 pints = 1 quart or 4 cups (32 oz)
8 quarts = 1 peck or 16 pints
4 pecks = 1 bushel or 32 quarts
4 quarts = 1 gallon
1 ounce = 28 grams
1/4 pound = 4 ounces
1 pound = 16 ounces
2.2 pounds = 1 kilogram (1000 grams)
12 inches = 1 foot or 30.48 centimeters
3 feet = 1 yard or .91 meters
144 square inches = 1 square foot
9 square feet = 1 square yard
1 mile = 1.6 kilometers
65 mph = 104.61 km/h
25 yard pool=1 length/1 lap
Olympic = 33 laps, Ironman = 85 laps

Times Table

	1	2	3	4	5	6	7	8	9	10	11	12
1	1	2	3	4	5	6	7	8	9	10	11	12
2	2	4	6	8	10	12	14	16	18	20	22	24
3	3	6	9	12	15	18	21	24	27	30	33	36
4	4	8	12	16	20	24	28	32	36	40	44	48
5	5	10	15	20	25	30	35	40	45	50	55	60
6	6	12	18	24	30	36	42	48	54	60	66	72
7	7	14	21	28	35	42	49	56	63	70	77	84
8	8	16	24	32	40	48	56	64	72	80	88	96
9	9	18	27	36	45	54	63	72	81	90	99	108
10	10	20	30	40	50	60	70	80	90	100	110	120
11	11	22	33	44	55	66	77	88	99	110	121	132
12	12	24	36	48	60	72	84	96	108	120	132	144

so iniquity shall not be your ruin. Ezekiel 18:30b

JANUARY 2020

Su	Mo	Tu	We	Th	Fr	Sa
			1	2	3	4
5	6	7	8	9	10	11
12	13	14	15	16	17	18
19	20	21	22	23	24	25
26	27	28	29	30	31	

FEBRUARY 2020

Su	Mo	Tu	We	Th	Fr	Sa
						1
2	3	4	5	6	7	8
9	10	11	12	13	14	15
16	17	18	19	20	21	22
23	24	25	26	27	28	29

MARCH 2020

Su	Mo	Tu	We	Th	Fr	Sa
1	2	3	4	5	6	7
8	9	10	11	12	13	14
15	16	17	18	19	20	21
22	23	24	25	26	27	28
29	30	31				

APRIL 2020

Su	Mo	Tu	We	Th	Fr	Sa
			1	2	3	4
5	6	7	8	9	10	11
12	13	14	15	16	17	18
19	20	21	22	23	24	25
26	27	28	29	30		

MAY 2020

Su	Mo	Tu	We	Th	Fr	Sa
					1	2
3	4	5	6	7	8	9
10	11	12	13	14	15	16
17	18	19	20	21	22	23
24	25	26	27	28	29	30
31						

JUNE 2020

Su	Mo	Tu	We	Th	Fr	Sa
	1	2	3	4	5	6
7	8	9	10	11	12	13
14	15	16	17	18	19	20
21	22	23	24	25	26	27
28	29	30				

JULY 2020

Su	Mo	Tu	We	Th	Fr	Sa
			1	2	3	4
5	6	7	8	9	10	11
12	13	14	15	16	17	18
19	20	21	22	23	24	25
26	27	28	29	30	31	

AUGUST 2020

Su	Mo	Tu	We	Th	Fr	Sa
						1
2	3	4	5	6	7	8
9	10	11	12	13	14	15
16	17	18	19	20	21	22
23	24	25	26	27	28	29
30	31					

SEPTEMBER 2020

Su	Mo	Tu	We	Th	Fr	Sa
		1	2	3	4	5
6	7	8	9	10	11	12
13	14	15	16	17	18	19
20	21	22	23	24	25	26
27	28	29	30			

OCTOBER 2020

Su	Mo	Tu	We	Th	Fr	Sa
				1	2	3
4	5	6	7	8	9	10
11	12	13	14	15	16	17
18	19	20	21	22	23	24
25	26	27	28	29	30	31

NOVEMBER 2020

Su	Mo	Tu	We	Th	Fr	Sa
1	2	3	4	5	6	7
8	9	10	11	12	13	14
15	16	17	18	19	20	21
22	23	24	25	26	27	28
29	30					

DECEMBER 2020

Su	Mo	Tu	We	Th	Fr	Sa
		1	2	3	4	5
6	7	8	9	10	11	12
13	14	15	16	17	18	19
20	21	22	23	24	25	26
27	28	29	30	31		

2020

As many as I love, I rebuke and chasten:

JANUARY 2021

Su	Mo	Tu	We	Th	Fr	Sa
					1	2
3	4	5	6	7	8	9
10	11	12	13	14	15	16
17	18	19	20	21	22	23
24	25	26	27	28	29	30
31						

FEBRUARY 2021

Su	Mo	Tu	We	Th	Fr	Sa
	1	2	3	4	5	6
7	8	9	10	11	12	13
14	15	16	17	18	19	20
21	22	23	24	25	26	27
28						

MARCH 2021

Su	Mo	Tu	We	Th	Fr	Sa
	1	2	3	4	5	6
7	8	9	10	11	12	13
14	15	16	17	18	19	20
21	22	23	24	25	26	27
28	29	30	31			

APRIL 2021

Su	Mo	Tu	We	Th	Fr	Sa
				1	2	3
4	5	6	7	8	9	10
11	12	13	14	15	16	17
18	19	20	21	22	23	24
25	26	27	28	29	30	

MAY 2021

Su	Mo	Tu	We	Th	Fr	Sa
						1
2	3	4	5	6	7	8
9	10	11	12	13	14	15
16	17	18	19	20	21	22
23	24	25	26	27	28	29
30	31					

JUNE 2021

Su	Mo	Tu	We	Th	Fr	Sa
		1	2	3	4	5
6	7	8	9	10	11	12
13	14	15	16	17	18	19
20	21	22	23	24	25	26
27	28	29	30			

JULY 2021

Su	Mo	Tu	We	Th	Fr	Sa
				1	2	3
4	5	6	7	8	9	10
11	12	13	14	15	16	17
18	19	20	21	22	23	24
25	26	27	28	29	30	31

AUGUST 2021

Su	Mo	Tu	We	Th	Fr	Sa
1	2	3	4	5	6	7
8	9	10	11	12	13	14
15	16	17	18	19	20	21
22	23	24	25	26	27	28
29	30	31				

SEPTEMBER 2021

Su	Mo	Tu	We	Th	Fr	Sa
			1	2	3	4
5	6	7	8	9	10	11
12	13	14	15	16	17	18
19	20	21	22	23	24	25
26	27	28	29	30		

OCTOBER 2021

Su	Mo	Tu	We	Th	Fr	Sa
					1	2
3	4	5	6	7	8	9
10	11	12	13	14	15	16
17	18	19	20	21	22	23
24	25	26	27	28	29	30
31						

NOVEMBER 2021

Su	Mo	Tu	We	Th	Fr	Sa
	1	2	3	4	5	6
7	8	9	10	11	12	13
14	15	16	17	18	19	20
21	22	23	24	25	26	27
28	29	30				

DECEMBER 2021

Su	Mo	Tu	We	Th	Fr	Sa
			1	2	3	4
5	6	7	8	9	10	11
12	13	14	15	16	17	18
19	20	21	22	23	24	25
26	27	28	29	30	31	

be zealous therefore, and repent. Revelation 3:19

JANUARY 2022

Su	Mo	Tu	We	Th	Fr	Sa
						1
2	3	4	5	6	7	8
9	10	11	12	13	14	15
16	17a	18	19	20	21	22
23	24	25	26	27	28	29
30	31					

FEBRUARY 2022

Su	Mo	Tu	We	Th	Fr	Sa
		1	2	3	4	5
6	7	8	9	10	11	12
13	14	15	16	17	18	19
20	21	22	23	24	25	26
27	28					

MARCH 2022

Su	Mo	Tu	We	Th	Fr	Sa
		1	2	3	4	5
6	7	8	9	10	11	12
13	14	15	16	17	18	19
20	21	22	23	24	25	26
27	28	29	30	31		

APRIL 2022

Su	Mo	Tu	We	Th	Fr	Sa
					1	2
3	4	5	6	7	8	9
10	11	12	13	14	15	16
17	18	19	20	21	22	23
24	25	26	27	28	29	30

MAY 2022

Su	Mo	Tu	We	Th	Fr	Sa
1	2	3	4	5	6	7
8	9	10	11	12	13	14
15	16	17	18	19	20	21
22	23	24	25	26	27	28
29	30	31				

JUNE 2022

Su	Mo	Tu	We	Th	Fr	Sa
			1	2	3	4
5	6	7	8	9	10	11
12	13	14	15	16	17	18
19	20	21	22	23	24	25
26	27	28	29	30		

JULY 2022

Su	Mo	Tu	We	Th	Fr	Sa
					1	2
3	4	5	6	7	8	9
10	11	12	13	14	15	16
17	18	19	20	21	22	23
24	25	26	27	28	29	30
31						

AUGUST 2022

Su	Mo	Tu	We	Th	Fr	Sa
	1	2	3	4	5	6
7	8	9	10	11	12	13
14	15	16	17	18	19	20
21	22	23	24	25	26	27
28	29	30	31			

SEPTEMBER 2022

Su	Mo	Tu	We	Th	Fr	Sa
				1	2	3
4	5	6	7	8	9	10
11	12	13	14	15	16	17
18	19	20	21	22	23	24
25	26	27	28	29	30	

OCTOBER 2022

Su	Mo	Tu	We	Th	Fr	Sa
						1
2	3	4	5	6	7	8
9	10	11	12	13	14	15
16	17	18	19	20	21	22
23	24	25	26	27	28	29
30	31					

NOVEMBER 2022

Su	Mo	Tu	We	Th	Fr	Sa
		1	2	3	4	5
6	7	8	9	10	11	12
13	14	15	16	17	18	19
20	21	22	23	24	25	26
27	28	29	30			

DECEMBER 2022

Su	Mo	Tu	We	Th	Fr	Sa
				1	2	3
4	5	6	7	8	9	10
11	12	13	14	15	16	17
18	19	20	21	22	23	24
25	26	27	28	29	30	31

82

Yet if any man suffer as a Christian, let him not be ashamed;

JANUARY 2023

Su	Mo	Tu	We	Th	Fr	Sa
1	2	3	4	5	6	7
8	9	10	11	12	13	14
15	16	17	18	19	20	21
22	23	24	25	26	27	28
29	30	31				

FEBRUARY 2023

Su	Mo	Tu	We	Th	Fr	Sa
			1	2	3	4
5	6	7	8	9	10	11
12	13	14	15	16	17	18
19	20	21	22	23	24	25
26	27	28				

MARCH 2023

Su	Mo	Tu	We	Th	Fr	Sa
			1	2	3	4
5	6	7	8	9	10	11
12	13	14	15	16	17	18
19	20	21	22	23	24	25
26	27	28	29	30	31	

APRIL 2023

Su	Mo	Tu	We	Th	Fr	Sa
						1
2	3	4	5	6	7	8
9	10	11	12	13	14	15
16	17	18	19	20	21	22
23	24	25	26	27	28	29
30						

MAY 2023

Su	Mo	Tu	We	Th	Fr	Sa
	1	2	3	4	5	6
7	8	9	10	11	12	13
14	15	16	17	18	19	20
21	22	23	24	25	26	27
28	29	30	31			

JUNE 2023

Su	Mo	Tu	We	Th	Fr	Sa
				1	2	3
4	5	6	7	8	9	10
11	12	13	14	15	16	17
18	19	20	21	22	23	24
25	26	27	28	29	30	

JULY 2023

Su	Mo	Tu	We	Th	Fr	Sa
						1
2	3	4	5	6	7	8
9	10	11	12	13	14	15
16	17	18	19	20	21	22
23	24	25	26	27	28	29
30	31					

AUGUST 2023

Su	Mo	Tu	We	Th	Fr	Sa
		1	2	3	4	5
6	7	8	9	10	11	12
13	14	15	16	17	18	19
20	21	22	23	24	25	26
27	28	29	30	31		

SEPTEMBER 2023

Su	Mo	Tu	We	Th	Fr	Sa
					1	2
3	4	5	6	7	8	9
10	11	12	13	14	15	16
17	18	19	20	21	22	23
24	25	26	27	28	29	30

OCTOBER 2023

Su	Mo	Tu	We	Th	Fr	Sa
1	2	3	4	5	6	7
8	9	10	11	12	13	14
15	16	17	18	19	20	21
22	23	24	25	26	27	28
29	30	31				

NOVEMBER 2023

Su	Mo	Tu	We	Th	Fr	Sa
			1	2	3	4
5	6	7	8	9	10	11
12	13	14	15	16	17	18
19	20	21	22	23	24	25
26	27	28	29	30		

DECEMBER 2023

Su	Mo	Tu	We	Th	Fr	Sa
					1	2
3	4	5	6	7	8	9
10	11	12	13	14	15	16
17	18	19	20	21	22	23
24	25	26	27	28	29	30
31						

2023

but let him glorify God on this behalf. 1 Peter 4:16

JANUARY 2024

Su	Mo	Tu	We	Th	Fr	Sa
	1	2	3	4	5	6
7	8	9	10	11	12	13
14	15	16	17	18	19	20
21	22	23	24	25	26	27
28	29	30	31			

FEBRUARY 2024

Su	Mo	Tu	We	Th	Fr	Sa
				1	2	3
4	5	6	7	8	9	10
11	12	13	14	15	16	17
18	19	20	21	22	23	24
25	26	27	28	29		

MARCH 2024

Su	Mo	Tu	We	Th	Fr	Sa
					1	2
3	4	5	6	7	8	9
10	11	12	13	14	15	16
17	18	19	20	21	22	23
24	25	26	27	28	29	30
31						

APRIL 2024

Su	Mo	Tu	We	Th	Fr	Sa
	1	2	3	4	5	6
7	8	9	10	11	12	13
14	15	16	17	18	19	20
21	22	23	24	25	26	27
28	29	30				

MAY 2024

Su	Mo	Tu	We	Th	Fr	Sa
			1	2	3	4
5	6	7	8	9	10	11
12	13	14	15	16	17	18
19	20	21	22	23	24	25
26	27	28	29	30	31	

JUNE 2024

Su	Mo	Tu	We	Th	Fr	Sa
						1
2	3	4	5	6	7	8
9	10	11	12	13	14	15
16	17	18	19	20	21	22
23	24	25	26	27	28	29
30						

JULY 2024

Su	Mo	Tu	We	Th	Fr	Sa
	1	2	3	4	5	6
7	8	9	10	11	12	13
14	15	16	17	18	19	20
21	22	23	24	25	26	27
28	29	30	31			

AUGUST 2024

Su	Mo	Tu	We	Th	Fr	Sa
				1	2	3
4	5	6	7	8	9	10
11	12	13	14	15	16	17
18	19	20	21	22	23	24
25	26	27	28	29	30	31

SEPTEMBER 2024

Su	Mo	Tu	We	Th	Fr	Sa
1	2	3	4	5	6	7
8	9	10	11	12	13	14
15	16	17	18	19	20	21
22	23	24	25	26	27	28
29	30					

OCTOBER 2024

Su	Mo	Tu	We	Th	Fr	Sa
		1	2	3	4	5
6	7	8	9	10	11	12
13	14	15	16	17	18	19
20	21	22	23	24	25	26
27	28	29	30	31		

NOVEMBER 2024

Su	Mo	Tu	We	Th	Fr	Sa
					1	2
3	4	5	6	7	8	9
10	11	12	13	14	15	16
17	18	19	20	21	22	23
24	25	26	27	28	29	30

DECEMBER 2024

Su	Mo	Tu	We	Th	Fr	Sa
1	2	3	4	5	6	7
8	9	10	11	12	13	14
15	16	17	18	19	20	21
22	23	24	25	26	27	28
29	30	31				

2024

84

For I know that my redeemer lives,

JANUARY 2025

Su	Mo	Tu	We	Th	Fr	Sa
			1	2	3	4
5	6	7	8	9	10	11
12	13	14	15	16	17	18
19	20	21	22	23	24	25
26	27	28	29	30	31	

FEBRUARY 2025

Su	Mo	Tu	We	Th	Fr	Sa
						1
2	3	4	5	6	7	8
9	10	11	12	13	14	15
16	17	18	19	20	21	22
23	24	25	26	27	28	

MARCH 2025

Su	Mo	Tu	We	Th	Fr	Sa
						1
2	3	4	5	6	7	8
9	10	11	12	13	14	15
16	17	18	19	20	21	22
23	24	25	26	27	28	29
30	31					

APRIL 2025

Su	Mo	Tu	We	Th	Fr	Sa
		1	2	3	4	5
6	7	8	9	10	11	12
13	14	15	16	17	18	19
20	21	22	23	24	25	26
27	28	29	30			

MAY 2025

Su	Mo	Tu	We	Th	Fr	Sa
				1	2	3
4	5	6	7	8	9	10
11	12	13	14	15	16	17
18	19	20	21	22	23	24
25	26	27	28	29	30	31

JUNE 2025

Su	Mo	Tu	We	Th	Fr	Sa
1	2	3	4	5	6	7
8	9	10	11	12	13	14
15	16	17	18	19	20	21
22	23	24	25	26	27	28
29	30					

JULY 2025

Su	Mo	Tu	We	Th	Fr	Sa
		1	2	3	4	5
6	7	8	9	10	11	12
13	14	15	16	17	18	19
20	21	22	23	24	25	26
27	28	29	30	31		

AUGUST 2025

Su	Mo	Tu	We	Th	Fr	Sa
					1	2
3	4	5	6	7	8	9
10	11	12	13	14	15	16
17	18	19	20	21	22	23
24	25	26	27	28	29	30
31						

SEPTEMBER 2025

Su	Mo	Tu	We	Th	Fr	Sa
	1	2	3	4	5	6
7	8	9	10	11	12	13
14	15	16	17	18	19	20
21	22	23	24	25	26	27
28	29	30				

OCTOBER 2025

Su	Mo	Tu	We	Th	Fr	Sa
			1	2	3	4
5	6	7	8	9	10	11
12	13	14	15	16	17	18
19	20	21	22	23	24	25
26	27	28	29	30	31	

NOVEMBER 2025

Su	Mo	Tu	We	Th	Fr	Sa
						1
2	3	4	5	6	7	8
9	10	11	12	13	14	15
16	17	18	19	20	21	22
23	24	25	26	27	28	29
30						

DECEMBER 2025

Su	Mo	Tu	We	Th	Fr	Sa
	1	2	3	4	5	6
7	8	9	10	11	12	13
14	15	16	17	18	19	20
21	22	23	24	25	26	27
28	29	30	31			

2025

and that he shall stand at the latter day upon the earth: Job 19:25

Month:_____

Sunday	Monday	Tuesday	Wednesday

Make your own Monthly Planner   *Don't write on this—*

Year:_____

Thursday	Friday	Saturday	Notes:

Use it as a master to photocopy or hand draw on plain paper.

87

YEARLY HOLIDAYS

Jan 1	New Year's Day
Sun on or before Jan 6	Epiphany (Magi—wise men visited Jesus)
3rd Mon in Jan or 1/15	Martin Luther King Day
Feb 2	Groundhog Day
Feb 12	Lincoln's Birthday
3rd Monday in Feb	President's Day
Feb 14	Valentine's Day
Feb 22	Washington's Day
46 days before Easter	Ash Wednesday (Beginning of 40 day fast)
Mar 17	St. Patrick's Day
15th thru 22nd of Hebrew Nissan	Passover
Sun before Easter	Palm Sunday
Thurs before Easter	Maundy Thursday (Last Supper)
Fri before Easter	Good Friday (Jesus crucified)
1st Sun after 1st full moon after spring Equinox	Resurrection Day / Easter (Jesus rose from the dead)
Apr 15	US Taxes due
Apr 16	Emancipation Day (Slaves free of servitude)
May 5	Cinco de Mayo (Mexican Army defeated French)
40 days after Easter	Ascension Day (Jesus taken up to heaven)
50 days after Easter	Pentecost (The Holy Spirit of God upon Believers)
2nd Sun in May	Mother's Day
3rd Sat	Armed Forces Day (Honor military forces)
Last Mon in May	Memorial Day (Remember soldiers who died)
Jun 14	Flag Day (Adoption of US flag in 1777)
Jun 19	Juneteenth (Announced abolition of slavery)
3rd Sun in Jun	Father's Day
Jul 4	Fourth of July (Declaration of Independence 1776)
1st Mon in Sep	Labor Day (Tribute to workers)
1st Sun after Labor Day	Grandparents Day
Sep 11	Patriot Day (Day of remembrance 9-11-2001)
2nd Mon in Oct	Columbus Day
Oct 31	All Hallows' Eve
1st Tue in Nov following 1st Mon	US Election Day
Nov 11	Veterans Day (Honor US Armed Forces)
4th Thr in Nov	Thanksgiving Day (Give thanks to God)
Dec 7	Pearl Harbor Day (Japanese attack on US WWII)
4th Sun before Christmas	Advent (Expectant and prep for Nativity of Jesus)
Dec 24	Christmas Eve
Dec 25	Christmas Day (Birth of Jesus the Christ, Lord, Savior)
Dec 26	Boxing Day (Servants receive gifts via Christmas box)
Dec 31	Watchnight (Review past year, confess, pray, resolve)
Leap Years	2024, 2028, 2032, 2036, 2040, 2044, 2048, 2052

For God has not given us the spirit of fear;

USA DAYLIGHT SAVINGS TIME — CHANGE CLOCKS AT 2:00 A.M.

Begins	Sunday, March 14, 2021	Begins	Sunday, March 10, 2024
Ends	Sunday, November 7, 2021	Ends	Sunday, November 3, 2024
Begins	Sunday, March 13, 2022	Begins	Sunday, March 9, 2025
Ends	Sunday, November 6, 2022	Ends	Sunday, November 2, 2025
Begins	Sunday, March 12, 2023	Begins	Sunday, March 8, 2026
Ends	Sunday, November 5, 202	Ends	Sunday, November 1, 2027

but of power, and of love, and of a sound mind.   2 Timothy 1:7

January

Su	M	T	W	Th	F	Sa
						1
2	3	4	5	6	7	8
9	10	11	12	13	14	15
16	17	18	19	20	21	22
23	24	25	26	27	28	29
30	31					

February

Su	M	T	W	Th	F	Sa
		1	2	3	4	5
6	7	8	9	10	11	12
13	14	15	16	17	18	19
20	21	22	23	24	25	26
27	28	29				

March

Su	M	T	W	Th	F	Sa
			1	2	3	4
5	6	7	8	9	10	11
12	13	14	15	16	17	18
19	20	21	22	23	24	25
26	27	28	29	30	31	

April

Su	M	T	W	Th	F	Sa
						1
2	3	4	5	6	7	8
9	10	11	12	13	14	15
16	17	18	19	20	21	22
23	24	25	26	27	28	29
30						

May

Su	M	T	W	Th	F	Sa
	1	2	3	4	5	6
7	8	9	10	11	12	13
14	15	16	17	18	19	20
21	22	23	24	25	26	27
28	29	30	31			

June

Su	M	T	W	Th	F	Sa
				1	2	3
4	5	6	7	8	9	10
11	12	13	14	15	16	17
18	19	20	21	22	23	24
25	26	27	28	29	30	

July

Su	M	T	W	Th	F	Sa
						1
2	3	4	5	6	7	8
9	10	11	12	13	14	15
16	17	18	19	20	21	22
23	24	25	26	27	28	29
30	31					

August

Su	M	T	W	Th	F	Sa
		1	2	3	4	5
6	7	8	9	10	11	12
13	14	15	16	17	18	19
20	21	22	23	24	25	26
27	28	29	30	31		

September

Su	M	T	W	Th	F	Sa
					1	2
3	4	5	6	7	8	9
10	11	12	13	14	15	16
17	18	19	20	21	22	23
24	25	26	27	28	29	30

October

Su	M	T	W	Th	F	Sa
1	2	3	4	5	6	7
8	9	10	11	12	13	14
15	16	17	18	19	20	21
22	23	24	25	26	27	28
29	30	31				

November

Su	M	T	W	Th	F	Sa
			1	2	3	4
5	6	7	8	9	10	11
12	13	14	15	16	17	18
19	20	21	22	23	24	25
26	27	28	29	30		

December

Su	M	T	W	Th	F	Sa
					1	2
3	4	5	6	7	8	9
10	11	12	13	14	15	16
17	18	19	20	21	22	23
24	25	26	27	28	29	30
31						

...For You, LORD, are good, and ready to forgive; and plenteous

CALENDAR for   1934 '45 '51 '62 '73 '79 '90
2001 '07 '18 '29 '35 '46 '57 '63

January

Su	M	T	W	Th	F	Sa
	1	2	3	4	5	6
7	8	9	10	11	12	13
14	15	16	17	18	19	20
21	22	23	24	25	26	27
28	29	30	31			

February

Su	M	T	W	Th	F	Sa
				1	2	3
4	5	6	7	8	9	10
11	12	13	14	15	16	17
18	19	20	21	22	23	24
25	26	27	28			

March

Su	M	T	W	Th	F	Sa
				1	2	3
4	5	6	7	8	9	10
11	12	13	14	15	16	17
18	19	20	21	22	23	24
25	26	27	28	29	30	31

April

Su	M	T	W	Th	F	Sa
1	2	3	4	5	6	7
8	9	10	11	12	13	14
15	16	17	18	19	20	21
22	23	24	25	26	27	28
29	30					

May

Su	M	T	W	Th	F	Sa
		1	2	3	4	5
6	7	8	9	10	11	12
13	14	15	16	17	18	19
20	21	22	23	24	25	26
27	28	29	30	31		

June

Su	M	T	W	Th	F	Sa
					1	2
3	4	5	6	7	8	9
10	11	12	13	14	15	16
17	18	19	20	21	22	23
24	25	26	27	28	29	30

July

Su	M	T	W	Th	F	Sa
1	2	3	4	5	6	7
8	9	10	11	12	13	14
15	16	17	18	19	20	21
22	23	24	25	26	27	28
29	30	31				

August

Su	M	T	W	Th	F	Sa
			1	2	3	4
5	6	7	8	9	10	11
12	13	14	15	16	17	18
19	20	21	22	23	24	25
26	27	28	29	30	31	

September

Su	M	T	W	Th	F	Sa
						1
2	3	4	5	6	7	8
9	10	11	12	13	14	15
16	17	18	19	20	21	22
23	24	25	26	27	28	29
30						

October

Su	M	T	W	Th	F	Sa
	1	2	3	4	5	6
7	8	9	10	11	12	13
14	15	16	17	18	19	20
21	22	23	24	25	26	27
28	29	30	31			

November

Su	M	T	W	Th	F	Sa
				1	2	3
4	5	6	7	8	9	10
11	12	13	14	15	16	17
18	19	20	21	22	23	24
25	26	27	28	29	30	

December

Su	M	T	W	Th	F	Sa
						1
2	3	4	5	6	7	8
9	10	11	12	13	14	15
16	17	18	19	20	21	22
23	24	25	26	27	28	29
30	31					

in mercy to all them that call upon You. Psalm 86:5   **91**

January

Su	M	T	W	Th	F	Sa
		1	2	3	4	5
6	7	8	9	10	11	12
13	14	15	16	17	18	19
20	21	22	23	24	25	26
27	28	29	30	31		

February

Su	M	T	W	Th	F	Sa
					1	2
3	4	5	6	7	8	9
10	11	12	13	14	15	16
17	18	19	20	21	22	23
24	25	26	27	28		

March

Su	M	T	W	Th	F	Sa
					1	2
3	4	5	6	7	8	9
10	11	12	13	14	15	16
17	18	19	20	21	22	23
24	25	26	27	28	29	30
31						

April

Su	M	T	W	Th	F	Sa
	1	2	3	4	5	6
7	8	9	10	11	12	13
14	15	16	17	18	19	20
21	22	23	24	25	26	27
28	29	30				

May

Su	M	T	W	Th	F	Sa
			1	2	3	4
5	6	7	8	9	10	11
12	13	14	15	16	17	18
19	20	21	22	23	24	25
26	27	28	29	30	31	

June

Su	M	T	W	Th	F	Sa
						1
2	3	4	5	6	7	8
9	10	11	12	13	14	15
16	17	18	19	20	21	22
23	24	25	26	27	28	29
30						

July

Su	M	T	W	Th	F	Sa
	1	2	3	4	5	6
7	8	9	10	11	12	13
14	15	16	17	18	19	20
21	22	23	24	25	26	27
28	29	30	31			

August

Su	M	T	W	Th	F	Sa
				1	2	3
4	5	6	7	8	9	10
11	12	13	14	15	16	17
18	19	20	21	22	23	24
25	26	27	28	29	30	31

September

Su	M	T	W	Th	F	Sa
1	2	3	4	5	6	7
8	9	10	11	12	13	14
15	16	17	18	19	20	21
22	23	24	25	26	27	28
29	30					

October

Su	M	T	W	Th	F	Sa
		1	2	3	4	5
6	7	8	9	10	11	12
13	14	15	16	17	18	19
20	21	22	23	24	25	26
27	28	29	30	31		

November

Su	M	T	W	Th	F	Sa
					1	2
3	4	5	6	7	8	9
10	11	12	13	14	15	16
17	18	19	20	21	22	23
24	25	26	27	28	29	30

December

Su	M	T	W	Th	F	Sa
1	2	3	4	5	6	7
8	9	10	11	12	13	14
15	16	17	18	19	20	21
22	23	24	25	26	27	28
29	30	31				

So then faith comes by hearing,

January

Su	M	T	W	Th	F	Sa
			1	2	3	4
5	6	7	8	9	10	11
12	13	14	15	16	17	18
19	20	21	22	23	24	25
26	27	28	29	30	31	

February

Su	M	T	W	Th	F	Sa
						1
2	3	4	5	6	7	8
9	10	11	12	13	14	15
16	17	18	19	20	21	22
23	24	25	26	27	28	

March

Su	M	T	W	Th	F	Sa
						1
2	3	4	5	6	7	8
9	10	11	12	13	14	15
16	17	18	19	20	21	22
23	24	25	26	27	28	29
30	31					

April

Su	M	T	W	Th	F	Sa
		1	2	3	4	5
6	7	8	9	10	11	12
13	14	15	16	17	18	19
20	21	22	23	24	25	26
27	28	29	30			

May

Su	M	T	W	Th	F	Sa
				1	2	3
4	5	6	7	8	9	10
11	12	13	14	15	16	17
18	19	20	21	22	23	24
25	26	27	28	29	30	31

June

Su	M	T	W	Th	F	Sa
1	2	3	4	5	6	7
8	9	10	11	12	13	14
15	16	17	18	19	20	21
22	23	24	25	26	27	28
29	30					

July

Su	M	T	W	Th	F	Sa
		1	2	3	4	5
6	7	8	9	10	11	12
13	14	15	16	17	18	19
20	21	22	23	24	25	26
27	28	29	30	31		

August

Su	M	T	W	Th	F	Sa
					1	2
3	4	5	6	7	8	9
10	11	12	13	14	15	16
17	18	19	20	21	22	23
24	25	26	27	28	29	30
31						

September

Su	M	T	W	Th	F	Sa
	1	2	3	4	5	6
7	8	9	10	11	12	13
14	15	16	17	18	19	20
21	22	23	24	25	26	27
28	29	30				

October

Su	M	T	W	Th	F	Sa
		1	2	3	4	
5	6	7	8	9	10	11
12	13	14	15	16	17	18
19	20	21	22	23	24	25
26	27	28	29	30	31	

November

Su	M	T	W	Th	F	Sa
						1
2	3	4	5	6	7	8
9	10	11	12	13	14	15
16	17	18	19	20	21	22
23	24	25	26	27	28	29
30						

December

Su	M	T	W	Th	F	Sa
	1	2	3	4	5	6
7	8	9	10	11	12	13
14	15	16	17	18	19	20
21	22	23	24	25	26	27
28	29	30	31			

and hearing by the word of God.   Romans 10:17   **93**

January

Su	M	T	W	Th	F	Sa
					1	2	3
4	5	6	7	8	9	10
11	12	13	14	15	16	17
18	19	20	21	22	23	24
25	26	27	28	29	30	31

February

Su	M	T	W	Th	F	Sa
1	2	3	4	5	6	7
8	9	10	11	12	13	14
15	16	17	18	19	20	21
22	23	24	25	26	27	28
29						

March

Su	M	T	W	Th	F	Sa
	1	2	3	4	5	6
7	8	9	10	11	12	13
14	15	16	17	18	19	20
21	22	23	24	25	26	27
28	29	30	31			

April

Su	M	T	W	Th	F	Sa
				1	2	3
4	5	6	7	8	9	10
11	12	13	14	15	16	17
18	19	20	21	22	23	24
25	26	27	28	29	30	

May

Su	M	T	W	Th	F	Sa
						1
2	3	4	5	6	7	8
9	10	11	12	13	14	15
16	17	18	19	20	21	22
23	24	25	26	27	28	29
30	31					

June

Su	M	T	W	Th	F	Sa
		1	2	3	4	5
6	7	8	9	10	11	12
13	14	15	16	17	18	19
20	21	22	23	24	25	26
27	28	29	30			

July

Su	M	T	W	Th	F	Sa
				1	2	3
4	5	6	7	8	9	10
11	12	13	14	15	16	17
18	19	20	21	22	23	24
25	26	27	28	29	30	31

August

Su	M	T	W	Th	F	Sa
1	2	3	4	5	6	7
8	9	10	11	12	13	14
15	16	17	18	19	20	21
22	23	24	25	26	27	28
29	30	31				

September

Su	M	T	W	Th	F	Sa
			1	2	3	4
5	6	7	8	9	10	11
12	13	14	15	16	17	18
19	20	21	22	23	24	25
26	27	28	29	30		

October

Su	M	T	W	Th	F	Sa
					1	2
3	4	5	6	7	8	9
10	11	12	13	14	15	16
17	18	19	20	21	22	23
24	25	26	27	28	29	30
31						

November

Su	M	T	W	Th	F	Sa
	1	2	3	4	5	6
7	8	9	10	11	12	13
14	15	16	17	18	19	20
21	22	23	24	25	26	27
28	29	30				

December

Su	M	T	W	Th	F	Sa
			1	2	3	4
5	6	7	8	9	10	11
12	13	14	15	16	17	18
19	20	21	22	23	24	25
26	27	28	29	30	31	

     The wisest man acccording to the Bible? _ _ _ _ _ _ _   1 Kings 3:12

CALENDAR for

January

Su	M	T	W	Th	F	Sa
						1
2	3	4	5	6	7	8
9	10	11	12	13	14	15
16	17	18	19	20	21	22
23	24	25	26	27	28	29
30	31					

February

Su	M	T	W	Th	F	Sa
		1	2	3	4	5
6	7	8	9	10	11	12
13	14	15	16	17	18	19
20	21	22	23	24	25	26
27	28					

March

Su	M	T	W	Th	F	Sa
		1	2	3	4	5
6	7	8	9	10	11	12
13	14	15	16	17	18	19
20	21	22	23	24	25	26
27	28	29	30	31		

April

Su	M	T	W	Th	F	Sa
					1	2
3	4	5	6	7	8	9
10	11	12	13	14	15	16
17	18	19	20	21	22	23
24	25	26	27	28	29	30

May

Su	M	T	W	Th	F	Sa
1	2	3	4	5	6	7
8	9	10	11	12	13	14
15	16	17	18	19	20	21
22	23	24	25	26	27	28
29	30	31				

June

Su	M	T	W	Th	F	Sa
			1	2	3	4	5
6	7	8	9	10	11	12
13	14	15	16	17	18	19
20	21	22	23	24	25	26
27	28	29	30			

July

Su	M	T	W	Th	F	Sa
					1	2
3	4	5	6	7	8	9
10	11	12	13	14	15	16
17	18	19	20	21	22	23
24	25	26	27	28	29	30
31						

August

Su	M	T	W	Th	F	Sa
	1	2	3	4	5	6
7	8	9	10	11	12	13
14	15	16	17	18	19	20
21	22	23	24	25	26	27
28	29	30	31			

September

Su	M	T	W	Th	F	Sa
				1	2	3
4	5	6	7	8	9	10
11	12	13	14	15	16	17
18	19	20	21	22	23	24
25	26	27	28	29	30	

October

Su	M	T	W	Th	F	Sa
						1
2	3	4	5	6	7	8
9	10	11	12	13	14	15
16	17	18	19	20	21	22
23	24	25	26	27	28	29
30	31					

November

Su	M	T	W	Th	F	Sa
		1	2	3	4	5
6	7	8	9	10	11	12
13	14	15	16	17	18	19
20	21	22	23	24	25	26
27	28	29	30			

December

Su	M	T	W	Th	F	Sa
				1	2	3	4
5	6	7	8	9	10	11
12	13	14	15	16	17	18
19	20	21	22	23	24	25
26	27	28	29	30	31	

Strongest man in the Bible? _ _ _ _ _ _   Judges 14, 15, 16 & Numbers 6:5 **95**

CALENDAR for 1933 '39 '50 '61 '67 '78 '89 '95
2006 '17 '23 '34 '45 '51 '62

January

Su	M	T	W	Th	F	Sa
1	2	3	4	5	6	7
8	9	10	11	12	13	14
15	16	17	18	19	20	21
22	23	24	25	26	27	28
29	30	31				

February

Su	M	T	W	Th	F	Sa
			1	2	3	4
5	6	7	8	9	10	11
12	13	14	15	16	17	18
19	20	21	22	23	24	25
26	27	28				

March

Su	M	T	W	Th	F	Sa
			1	2	3	4
5	6	7	8	9	10	11
12	13	14	15	16	17	18
19	20	21	22	23	24	25
26	27	28	29	30	31	

April

Su	M	T	W	Th	F	Sa
						1
2	3	4	5	6	7	8
9	10	11	12	13	14	15
16	17	18	19	20	21	22
23	24	25	26	27	28	29
30						

May

Su	M	T	W	Th	F	Sa
	1	2	3	4	5	6
7	8	9	10	11	12	13
14	15	16	17	18	19	20
21	22	23	24	25	26	27
28	29	30	31			

June

Su	M	T	W	Th	F	Sa
				1	2	3
4	5	6	7	8	9	10
11	12	13	14	15	16	17
18	19	20	21	22	23	24
25	26	27	28	29	30	

July

Su	M	T	W	Th	F	Sa
						1
2	3	4	5	6	7	8
9	10	11	12	13	14	15
16	17	18	19	20	21	22
23	24	25	26	27	28	29
30	31					

August

Su	M	T	W	Th	F	Sa
		1	2	3	4	5
6	7	8	9	10	11	12
13	14	15	16	17	18	19
20	21	22	23	24	25	26
27	28	29	30	31		

September

Su	M	T	W	Th	F	Sa
					1	2
3	4	5	6	7	8	9
10	11	12	13	14	15	16
17	18	19	20	21	22	23
24	25	26	27	28	29	30

October

Su	M	T	W	Th	F	Sa
1	2	3	4	5	6	7
8	9	10	11	12	13	14
15	16	17	18	19	20	21
22	23	24	25	26	27	28
29	30	31				

November

Su	M	T	W	Th	F	Sa
			1	2	3	4
5	6	7	8	9	10	11
12	13	14	15	16	17	18
19	20	21	22	23	24	25
26	27	28	29	30		

December

Su	M	T	W	Th	F	Sa
					1	2
3	4	5	6	7	8	9
10	11	12	13	14	15	16
17	18	19	20	21	22	23
24	25	26	27	28	29	30
31						

Riddle: Before Boaz got married, what kind of man was he?

January

Su	M	T	W	Th	F	Sa
		1	2	3	4	5
6	7	8	9	10	11	12
13	14	15	16	17	18	19
20	21	22	23	24	25	26
27	28	29	30	31		

February

Su	M	T	W	Th	F	Sa
					1	2
3	4	5	6	7	8	9
10	11	12	13	14	15	16
17	18	19	20	21	22	23
24	25	26	27	28	29	

March

Su	M	T	W	Th	F	Sa
						1
2	3	4	5	6	7	8
9	10	11	12	13	14	15
16	17	18	19	20	21	22
23	24	25	26	27	28	29
30	31					

April

Su	M	T	W	Th	F	Sa
		1	2	3	4	5
6	7	8	9	10	11	12
13	14	15	16	17	18	19
20	21	22	23	24	25	26
27	28	29	30			

May

Su	M	T	W	Th	F	Sa
				1	2	3
4	5	6	7	8	9	10
11	12	13	14	15	16	17
18	19	20	21	22	23	24
25	26	27	28	29	30	31

June

Su	M	T	W	Th	F	Sa
1	2	3	4	5	6	7
8	9	10	11	12	13	14
15	16	17	18	19	20	21
22	23	24	25	26	27	28
29	30					

July

Su	M	T	W	Th	F	Sa
		1	2	3	4	5
6	7	8	9	10	11	12
13	14	15	16	17	18	19
20	21	22	23	24	25	26
27	28	29	30	31		

August

Su	M	T	W	Th	F	Sa
					1	2
3	4	5	6	7	8	9
10	11	12	13	14	15	16
17	18	19	20	21	22	23
24	25	26	27	28	29	30
31						

September

Su	M	T	W	Th	F	Sa
	1	2	3	4	5	6
7	8	9	10	11	12	13
14	15	16	17	18	19	20
21	22	23	24	25	26	27
28	29	30				

October

Su	M	T	W	Th	F	Sa
		1	2	3		4
5	6	7	8	9	10	11
12	13	14	15	16	17	18
19	20	21	22	23	24	25
26	27	28	29	30	31	

November

Su	M	T	W	Th	F	Sa
						1
2	3	4	5	6	7	8
9	10	11	12	13	14	15
16	17	18	19	20	21	22
23	24	25	26	27	28	29
30						

December

Su	M	T	W	Th	F	Sa
	1	2	3	4	5	6
7	8	9	10	11	12	13
14	15	16	17	18	19	20
21	22	23	24	25	26	27
28	29	30	31			

January

Su	M	T	W	Th	F	Sa
					1	2	3
4	5	6	7	8	9	10
11	12	13	14	15	16	17
18	19	20	21	22	23	24
25	26	27	28	29	30	31

February

Su	M	T	W	Th	F	Sa
1	2	3	4	5	6	7
8	9	10	11	12	13	14
15	16	17	18	19	20	21
22	23	24	25	26	27	28

March

Su	M	T	W	Th	F	Sa
1	2	3	4	5	6	7
8	9	10	11	12	13	14
15	16	17	18	19	20	21
22	23	24	25	26	27	28
29	30	31				

April

Su	M	T	W	Th	F	Sa
			1	2	3	4
5	6	7	8	9	10	11
12	13	14	15	16	17	18
19	20	21	22	23	24	25
26	27	28	29	30		

May

Su	M	T	W	Th	F	Sa
					1	2
3	4	5	6	7	8	9
10	11	12	13	14	15	16
17	18	19	20	21	22	23
24	25	26	27	28	29	30
31						

June

Su	M	T	W	Th	F	Sa
	1	2	3	4	5	6
7	8	9	10	11	12	13
14	15	16	17	18	19	20
21	22	23	24	25	26	27
28	29	30				

July

Su	M	T	W	Th	F	Sa
			1	2	3	4
5	6	7	8	9	10	11
12	13	14	15	16	17	18
19	20	21	22	23	24	25
26	27	28	29	30	31	

August

Su	M	T	W	Th	F	Sa
						1
2	3	4	5	6	7	8
9	10	11	12	13	14	15
16	17	18	19	20	21	22
23	24	25	26	27	28	29
30	31					

September

Su	M	T	W	Th	F	Sa
		1	2	3	4	5
6	7	8	9	10	11	12
13	14	15	16	17	18	19
20	21	22	23	24	25	26
27	28	29	30			

October

Su	M	T	W	Th	F	Sa
				1	2	3
4	5	6	7	8	9	10
11	12	13	14	15	16	17
18	19	20	21	22	23	24
25	26	27	28	29	30	31

November

Su	M	T	W	Th	F	Sa
1	2	3	4	5	6	7
8	9	10	11	12	13	14
15	16	17	18	19	20	21
22	23	24	25	26	27	28
29	30					

December

Su	M	T	W	Th	F	Sa
		1	2	3	4	5
6	7	8	9	10	11	12
13	14	15	16	17	18	19
20	21	22	23	24	25	26
27	28	29	30	31		

The longest word in the Bible is

January

Su	M	T	W	Th	F	Sa
					1	2
3	4	5	6	7	8	9
10	11	12	13	14	15	16
17	18	19	20	21	22	23
24	25	26	27	28	29	30
31						

February

Su	M	T	W	Th	F	Sa
	1	2	3	4	5	6
7	8	9	10	11	12	13
14	15	16	17	18	19	20
21	22	23	24	25	26	27
28						

March

Su	M	T	W	Th	F	Sa
	1	2	3	4	5	6
7	8	9	10	11	12	13
14	15	16	17	18	19	20
21	22	23	24	25	26	27
28	29	30	31			

April

Su	M	T	W	Th	F	Sa
				1	2	3
4	5	6	7	8	9	10
11	12	13	14	15	16	17
18	19	20	21	22	23	24
25	26	27	28	29	30	

May

Su	M	T	W	Th	F	Sa
						1
2	3	4	5	6	7	8
9	10	11	12	13	14	15
16	17	18	19	20	21	22
23	24	25	26	27	28	29
30	31					

June

Su	M	T	W	Th	F	Sa
		1	2	3	4	5
6	7	8	9	10	11	12
13	14	15	16	17	18	19
20	21	22	23	24	25	26
27	28	29	30			

July

Su	M	T	W	Th	F	Sa
				1	2	3
4	5	6	7	8	9	10
11	12	13	14	15	16	17
18	19	20	21	22	23	24
25	26	27	28	29	30	31

August

Su	M	T	W	Th	F	Sa
1	2	3	4	5	6	7
8	9	10	11	12	13	14
15	16	17	18	19	20	21
22	23	24	25	26	27	28
29	30	31				

September

Su	M	T	W	Th	F	Sa
			1	2	3	4
5	6	7	8	9	10	11
12	13	14	15	16	17	18
19	20	21	22	23	24	25
26	27	28	29	30		

October

Su	M	T	W	Th	F	Sa
					1	2
3	4	5	6	7	8	9
10	11	12	13	14	15	16
17	18	19	20	21	22	23
24	25	26	27	28	29	30
31						

November

Su	M	T	W	Th	F	Sa
	1	2	3	4	5	6
7	8	9	10	11	12	13
14	15	16	17	18	19	20
21	22	23	24	25	26	27
28	29	30				

December

Su	M	T	W	Th	F	Sa
			1	2	3	4
5	6	7	8	9	10	11
12	13	14	15	16	17	18
19	20	21	22	23	24	25
26	27	28	29	30	31	

Isaiah 8:3

January

Su	M	T	W	Th	F	Sa
1	2	3	4	5	6	7
8	9	10	11	12	13	14
15	16	17	18	19	20	21
22	23	24	25	26	27	28
29	30	31				

February

Su	M	T	W	Th	F	Sa
			1	2	3	4
5	6	7	8	9	10	11
12	13	14	15	16	17	18
19	20	21	22	23	24	25
26	27	28	29			

March

Su	M	T	W	Th	F	Sa
				1	2	3
4	5	6	7	8	9	10
11	12	13	14	15	16	17
18	19	20	21	22	23	24
25	26	27	28	29	30	31

April

Su	M	T	W	Th	F	Sa
1	2	3	4	5	6	7
8	9	10	11	12	13	14
15	16	17	18	19	20	21
22	23	24	25	26	27	28
29	30					

May

Su	M	T	W	Th	F	Sa
		1	2	3	4	5
6	7	8	9	10	11	12
13	14	15	16	17	18	19
20	21	22	23	24	25	26
27	28	29	30	31		

June

Su	M	T	W	Th	F	Sa
					1	2
3	4	5	6	7	8	9
10	11	12	13	14	15	16
17	18	19	20	21	22	23
24	25	26	27	28	29	30

July

Su	M	T	W	Th	F	Sa
1	2	3	4	5	6	7
8	9	10	11	12	13	14
15	16	17	18	19	20	21
22	23	24	25	26	27	28
29	30	31				

August

Su	M	T	W	Th	F	Sa
			1	2	3	4
5	6	7	8	9	10	11
12	13	14	15	16	17	18
19	20	21	22	23	24	25
26	27	28	29	30	31	

September

Su	M	T	W	Th	F	Sa
						1
2	3	4	5	6	7	8
9	10	11	12	13	14	15
16	17	18	19	20	21	22
23	24	25	26	27	28	29
30						

October

Su	M	T	W	Th	F	Sa
	1	2	3	4	5	6
7	8	9	10	11	12	13
14	15	16	17	18	19	20
21	22	23	24	25	26	27
28	29	30	31			

November

Su	M	T	W	Th	F	Sa
				1	2	3
4	5	6	7	8	9	10
11	12	13	14	15	16	17
18	19	20	21	22	23	24
25	26	27	28	29	30	

December

Su	M	T	W	Th	F	Sa
						1
2	3	4	5	6	7	8
9	10	11	12	13	14	15
16	17	18	19	20	21	22
23	24	25	26	27	28	29
30	31					

The world's largest Bible is 43.5" tall, 98" wide and 34" thick. Finished

January

Su	M	T	W	Th	F	Sa
					1	2
3	4	5	6	7	8	9
10	11	12	13	14	15	16
17	18	19	20	21	22	23
24	25	26	27	28	29	30
31						

February

Su	M	T	W	Th	F	Sa
	1	2	3	4	5	6
7	8	9	10	11	12	13
14	15	16	17	18	19	20
21	22	23	24	25	26	27
28	29					

March

Su	M	T	W	Th	F	Sa
		1	2	3	4	5
6	7	8	9	10	11	12
13	14	15	16	17	18	19
20	21	22	23	24	25	26
27	28	29	30	31		

April

Su	M	T	W	Th	F	Sa
					1	2
3	4	5	6	7	8	9
10	11	12	13	14	15	16
17	18	19	20	21	22	23
24	25	26	27	28	29	30

May

Su	M	T	W	Th	F	Sa
1	2	3	4	5	6	7
8	9	10	11	12	13	14
15	16	17	18	19	20	21
22	23	24	25	26	27	28
29	30	31				

June

Su	M	T	W	Th	F	Sa
			1	2	3	4
5	6	7	8	9	10	11
12	13	14	15	16	17	18
19	20	21	22	23	24	25
26	27	28	29	30		

July

Su	M	T	W	Th	F	Sa
					1	2
3	4	5	6	7	8	9
10	11	12	13	14	15	16
17	18	19	20	21	22	23
24	25	26	27	28	29	30
31						

August

Su	M	T	W	Th	F	Sa
	1	2	3	4	5	6
7	8	9	10	11	12	13
14	15	16	17	18	19	20
21	22	23	24	25	26	27
28	29	30	31			

September

Su	M	T	W	Th	F	Sa
				1	2	3
4	5	6	7	8	9	10
11	12	13	14	15	16	17
18	19	20	21	22	23	24
25	26	27	28	29	30	

October

Su	M	T	W	Th	F	Sa
						1
2	3	4	5	6	7	8
9	10	11	12	13	14	15
16	17	18	19	20	21	22
23	24	25	26	27	28	29
30	31					

November

Su	M	T	W	Th	F	Sa
		1	2	3	4	5
6	7	8	9	10	11	12
13	14	15	16	17	18	19
20	21	22	23	24	25	26
27	28	29	30			

December

Su	M	T	W	Th	F	Sa
				1	2	3
4	5	6	7	8	9	10
11	12	13	14	15	16	17
18	19	20	21	22	23	24
25	26	27	28	29	30	31

January

Su	M	T	W	Th	F	Sa
			1	2	3	4
5	6	7	8	9	10	11
12	13	14	15	16	17	18
19	20	21	22	23	24	25
26	27	28	29	30	31	

February

Su	M	T	W	Th	F	Sa
						1
2	3	4	5	6	7	8
9	10	11	12	13	14	15
16	17	18	19	20	21	22
23	24	25	26	27	28	29

March

Su	M	T	W	Th	F	Sa
1	2	3	4	5	6	7
8	9	10	11	12	13	14
15	16	17	18	19	20	21
22	23	24	25	26	27	28
29	30	31				

April

Su	M	T	W	Th	F	Sa
			1	2	3	4
5	6	7	8	9	10	11
12	13	14	15	16	17	18
19	20	21	22	23	24	25
26	27	28	29	30		

May

Su	M	T	W	Th	F	Sa
					1	2
3	4	5	6	7	8	9
10	11	12	13	14	15	16
17	18	19	20	21	22	23
24	25	26	27	28	29	30
31						

June

Su	M	T	W	Th	F	Sa
	1	2	3	4	5	6
7	8	9	10	11	12	13
14	15	16	17	18	19	20
21	22	23	24	25	26	27
28	29	30				

July

Su	M	T	W	Th	F	Sa
			1	2	3	4
5	6	7	8	9	10	11
12	13	14	15	16	17	18
19	20	21	22	23	24	25
26	27	28	29	30	31	

August

Su	M	T	W	Th	F	Sa
						1
2	3	4	5	6	7	8
9	10	11	12	13	14	15
16	17	18	19	20	21	22
23	24	25	26	27	28	29
30	31					

September

Su	M	T	W	Th	F	Sa
		1	2	3	4	5
6	7	8	9	10	11	12
13	14	15	16	17	18	19
20	21	22	23	24	25	26
27	28	29	30			

October

Su	M	T	W	Th	F	Sa
				1	2	3
4	5	6	7	8	9	10
11	12	13	14	15	16	17
18	19	20	21	22	23	24
25	26	27	28	29	30	31

November

Su	M	T	W	Th	F	Sa
1	2	3	4	5	6	7
8	9	10	11	12	13	14
15	16	17	18	19	20	21
22	23	24	25	26	27	28
29	30					

December

Su	M	T	W	Th	F	Sa
		1	2	3	4	5
6	7	8	9	10	11	12
13	14	15	16	17	18	19
20	21	22	23	24	25	26
27	28	29	30	31		

What does it mean to be "born again"?

January

Su	M	T	W	Th	F	Sa
	1	2	3	4	5	6
7	8	9	10	11	12	13
14	15	16	17	18	19	20
21	22	23	24	25	26	27
28	29	30	31			

February

Su	M	T	W	Th	F	Sa
				1	2	3
4	5	6	7	8	9	10
11	12	13	14	15	16	17
18	19	20	21	22	23	24
25	26	27	28	29		

March

Su	M	T	W	Th	F	Sa
					1	2
3	4	5	6	7	8	9
10	11	12	13	14	15	16
17	18	19	20	21	22	23
24	25	26	27	28	29	30
31						

April

Su	M	T	W	Th	F	Sa
	1	2	3	4	5	6
7	8	9	10	11	12	13
14	15	16	17	18	19	20
21	22	23	24	25	26	27
28	29	30				

May

Su	M	T	W	Th	F	Sa
			1	2	3	4
5	6	7	8	9	10	11
12	13	14	15	16	17	18
19	20	21	22	23	24	25
26	27	28	29	30	31	

June

Su	M	T	W	Th	F	Sa
						1
2	3	4	5	6	7	8
9	10	11	12	13	14	15
16	17	18	19	20	21	22
23	24	25	26	27	28	29
30						

July

Su	M	T	W	Th	F	Sa
	1	2	3	4	5	6
7	8	9	10	11	12	13
14	15	16	17	18	19	20
21	22	23	24	25	26	27
28	29	30	31			

August

Su	M	T	W	Th	F	Sa
				1	2	3
4	5	6	7	8	9	10
11	12	13	14	15	16	17
18	19	20	21	22	23	24
25	26	27	28	29	30	31

September

Su	M	T	W	Th	F	Sa
1	2	3	4	5	6	7
8	9	10	11	12	13	14
15	16	17	18	19	20	21
22	23	24	25	26	27	28
29	30					

October

Su	M	T	W	Th	F	Sa
		1	2	3	4	5
6	7	8	9	10	11	12
13	14	15	16	17	18	19
20	21	22	23	24	25	26
27	28	29	30	31		

November

Su	M	T	W	Th	F	Sa
					1	2
3	4	5	6	7	8	9
10	11	12	13	14	15	16
17	18	19	20	21	22	23
24	25	26	27	28	29	30

December

Su	M	T	W	Th	F	Sa
1	2	3	4	5	6	7
8	9	10	11	12	13	14
15	16	17	18	19	20	21
22	23	24	25	26	27	28
29	30	31				

Figure it out by reading John 3, 4, & 5, then 2 Corinthians 5:17   **103**

BEST BOOKS OF ALL TIME

1_____
2_____
3_____
4_____
5_____
6_____
7_____
8_____
9_____
10_____
11_____
12_____
13_____
14_____
15_____
16_____
17_____
18_____
19_____
20_____
21_____
22_____
23_____
24_____
25_____
26_____
27_____
28_____
29_____
30_____
31_____
32_____
33_____
34_____
35_____

36_____
37_____
38_____
39_____
40_____
41_____
42_____
43_____
44_____
45_____
46_____
47_____
48_____
49_____
50_____
51_____
52_____
53_____
54_____
55_____
56_____
57_____
58_____
59_____
60_____
61_____
62_____
63_____
64_____
65_____
66_____
67_____
68_____
69_____
70_____

Behold, the eye of the LORD is upon them that fear him,

BEST DECISIONS I'VE EVER MADE

1 _____

_____

2 _____

_____

3 _____

_____

4 _____

_____

5 _____

_____

6 _____

_____

7 _____

_____

8 _____

_____

9 _____

_____

10_____

_____

11_____

_____

12_____

_____

13_____

_____

14_____

_____

15_____

_____

16_____

_____

upon them that hope in his mercy; Psalm 33:18

BEST SHOWS OR MOVIES OF ALL TIME

1_____
2_____
3_____
4_____
5_____
6_____
7_____
8_____
9_____
10_____
11_____
12_____
13_____
14_____
15_____
16_____
17_____
18_____
19_____
20_____
21_____
22_____
23_____
24_____
25_____
26_____
27_____
28_____
29_____
30_____
31_____
32_____
33_____
34_____
35_____

36_____
37_____
38_____
39_____
40_____
41_____
42_____
43_____
44_____
45_____
46_____
47_____
48_____
49_____
50_____
51_____
52_____
53_____
54_____
55_____
56_____
57_____
58_____
59_____
60_____
61_____
62_____
63_____
64_____
65_____
66_____
67_____
68_____
69_____
70_____

...My peace I give to you: not as the world gives, give I to you.

BOOKS TO READ & SHOWS OR MOVIES TO SEE

1 _____
2 _____
3 _____
4 _____
5 _____
6 _____
7 _____
8 _____
9 _____
10 _____
11 _____
12 _____
13 _____
14 _____
15 _____
16 _____
17 _____
18 _____
19 _____
20 _____
21 _____
22 _____
23 _____
24 _____
25 _____
26 _____
27 _____
28 _____
29 _____
30 _____
31 _____
32 _____
33 _____
34 _____
35 _____

36 _____
37 _____
38 _____
39 _____
40 _____
41 _____
42 _____
43 _____
44 _____
45 _____
46 _____
47 _____
48 _____
49 _____
50 _____
51 _____
52 _____
53 _____
54 _____
55 _____
56 _____
57 _____
58 _____
59 _____
60 _____
61 _____
62 _____
63 _____
64 _____
65 _____
66 _____
67 _____
68 _____
69 _____
70 _____

Let not your heart be troubled, neither let it be afraid. John 14:27b

CHECKLIST

☐ _____
☐ _____
☐ _____
☐ _____
☐ _____
☐ _____
☐ _____
☐ _____
☐ _____
☐ _____
☐ _____
☐ _____
☐ _____
☐ _____
☐ _____
☐ _____
☐ _____
☐ _____
☐ _____
☐ _____
☐ _____
☐ _____
☐ _____
☐ _____
☐ _____
☐ _____
☐ _____
☐ _____
☐ _____
☐ _____
☐ _____
☐ _____
☐ _____
☐ _____

☐ _____
☐ _____
☐ _____
☐ _____
☐ _____
☐ _____
☐ _____
☐ _____
☐ _____
☐ _____
☐ _____
☐ _____
☐ _____
☐ _____
☐ _____
☐ _____
☐ _____
☐ _____
☐ _____
☐ _____
☐ _____
☐ _____
☐ _____
☐ _____
☐ _____
☐ _____
☐ _____
☐ _____
☐ _____
☐ _____
☐ _____
☐ _____
☐ _____
☐ _____

Verily, verily, I say unto you, Except a man be born of water and of

GOOD DECISIONS I STILL HAVE TIME TO MAKE

1 _____ ❏

2 _____ ❏

3 _____ ❏

4 _____ ❏

5 _____ ❏

6 _____ ❏

7 _____ ❏

8 _____ ❏

9 _____ ❏

10 _____ ❏

11 _____ ❏

12 _____ ❏

13 _____ ❏

14 _____ ❏

15 _____ ❏

16 _____ ❏

the Spirit, he cannot enter into the kingdom of God. John 3:5

HOPE/WISH LIST

1 _____
2 _____
3 _____
4 _____
5 _____
6 _____
7 _____
8 _____
9 _____
10 _____
11 _____
12 _____
13 _____
14 _____
15 _____
16 _____
17 _____
18 _____
19 _____
20 _____
21 _____
22 _____
23 _____
24 _____
25 _____
26 _____
27 _____
28 _____
29 _____
30 _____
31 _____
32 _____
33 _____
34 _____
35 _____

36 _____
37 _____
38 _____
39 _____
40 _____
41 _____
42 _____
43 _____
44 _____
45 _____
46 _____
47 _____
48 _____
49 _____
50 _____
51 _____
52 _____
53 _____
54 _____
55 _____
56 _____
57 _____
58 _____
59 _____
60 _____
61 _____
62 _____
63 _____
64 _____
65 _____
66 _____
67 _____
68 _____
69 _____
70 _____

He that has the Son has life;

INVENTIONS I WISH WERE MADE

1_____
2_____
3_____
4_____
5_____
6_____
7_____
8_____
9_____
10_____
11_____
12_____
13_____
14_____
15_____
16_____
17_____
18_____
19_____
20_____
21_____
22_____
23_____
24_____
25_____
26_____
27_____
28_____
29_____
30_____
31_____
32_____
33_____
34_____
35_____

36_____
37_____
38_____
39_____
40_____
41_____
42_____
43_____
44_____
45_____
46_____
47_____
48_____
49_____
50_____
51_____
52_____
53_____
54_____
55_____
56_____
57_____
58_____
59_____
60_____
61_____
62_____
63_____
64_____
65_____
66_____
67_____
68_____
69_____
70_____

and he that has not the Son of God has not life. 1 John 5:12

MY BUCKET LIST

1. _____ ❏
2. _____ ❏
3. _____ ❏
4. _____ ❏
5. _____ ❏
6. _____ ❏
7. _____ ❏
8. _____ ❏
9. _____ ❏
10. _____ ❏
11. _____ ❏
12. _____ ❏
13. _____ ❏
14. _____ ❏
15. _____ ❏
16. _____ ❏
17. _____ ❏
18. _____ ❏
19. _____ ❏
20. _____ ❏
21. _____ ❏
22. _____ ❏
23. _____ ❏
24. _____ ❏
25. _____ ❏

If we say that we have not sinned, we make him a liar,

26 _____ ❑

27 _____ ❑

28 _____ ❑

29 _____ ❑

30 _____ ❑

31 _____ ❑

32 _____ ❑

33 _____ ❑

34 _____ ❑

35 _____ ❑

36 _____ ❑

37 _____ ❑

38 _____ ❑

39 _____ ❑

40 _____ ❑

41 _____ ❑

42 _____ ❑

43 _____ ❑

44 _____ ❑

45 _____ ❑

46 _____ ❑

47 _____ ❑

48 _____ ❑

49 _____ ❑

50 _____ ❑

51 _____ ❏

52 _____ ❏

53 _____ ❏

54 _____ ❏

55 _____ ❏

56 _____ ❏

57 _____ ❏

58 _____ ❏

59 _____ ❏

60 _____ ❏

61 _____ ❏

62 _____ ❏

63 _____ ❏

64 _____ ❏

65 _____ ❏

66 _____ ❏

67 _____ ❏

68 _____ ❏

69 _____ ❏

70 _____ ❏

71 _____ ❏

72 _____ ❏

73 _____ ❏

74 _____ ❏

75 _____ ❏

The Bible mentions left-handed people. True or False?

76 _____ ❏

77 _____ ❏

78 _____ ❏

79 _____ ❏

80 _____ ❏

81 _____ ❏

82 _____ ❏

83 _____ ❏

84 _____ ❏

85 _____ ❏

86 _____ ❏

87 _____ ❏

88 _____ ❏

89 _____ ❏

90 _____ ❏

91 _____ ❏

92 _____ ❏

93 _____ ❏

94 _____ ❏

95 _____ ❏

96 _____ ❏

97 _____ ❏

98 _____ ❏

99 _____ ❏

100 _____ ❏

101 _____ ❏

Look it up: Judges 3 & Judges 20

MY GOAL PLANNER

ADVENTURE GOALS

1 ☐ _____ _____
2 ☐ _____ _____
3 ☐ _____ _____

BREAK BAD HABIT GOALS

1 ☐ _____ _____
2 ☐ _____ _____
3 ☐ _____ _____

CREATIVE GOALS

1 ☐ _____ _____
2 ☐ _____ _____
3 ☐ _____ _____

EDUCATIONAL GOALS

1 ☐ _____ _____
2 ☐ _____ _____
3 ☐ _____ _____

FAMILY GOALS

1 ☐ _____ _____
2 ☐ _____ _____
3 ☐ _____ _____

FINANCIAL GOALS

1 ☐ _____ _____
2 ☐ _____ _____
3 ☐ _____ _____

FITNESS GOALS

1 ☐ _____ _____
2 ☐ _____ _____
3 ☐ _____ _____

JOB/CAREER/VOCATION/BUSINESS GOALS

1 ☐ _____ _____
2 ☐ _____ _____
3 ☐ _____ _____

I can do all things through Christ

MY GOAL PLANNER

SOCIAL GOALS   Month/Year

1 ☐ _____   _____
2 ☐ _____   _____
3 ☐ _____   _____

SPIRITUAL GOALS

1 ☐ _____   _____
2 ☐ _____   _____
3 ☐ _____   _____

START GOOD HABIT GOALS

1 ☐ _____   _____
2 ☐ _____   _____
3 ☐ _____   _____

TIME MANAGEMENT GOALS

1 ☐ _____   _____
2 ☐ _____   _____
3 ☐ _____   _____

TRAVELING GOALS

1 ☐ _____   _____
2 ☐ _____   _____
3 ☐ _____   _____

VOLUNTEERING GOALS

1 ☐ _____   _____
2 ☐ _____   _____
3 ☐ _____   _____

OTHER GOALS

1 ☐ _____   _____
2 ☐ _____   _____
3 ☐ _____   _____
4 ☐ _____   _____
5 ☐ _____   _____
6 ☐ _____   _____
7 ☐ _____   _____

which strengthens me. Philippians 4:13   **117**

MY ULTIMATE GOAL

List your #1 ultimate goal, then work backwards from the bottom up.

Month/Year

25 _____ _____

24 _____ _____

23 _____ _____

22 _____ _____

21 _____ _____

20 _____ _____

19 _____ _____

18 _____ _____

17 _____ _____

16 _____ _____

15 _____ _____

14 _____ _____

13 _____ _____

12 _____ _____

11 _____ _____

10 _____ _____

9 _____ _____

8 _____ _____

7 _____ _____

6 _____ _____

5 _____ _____

4 _____ _____

3 _____ _____

2 _____ _____

#1 _____ _____

What do you have to do to reach your goal? *Fill in #1, then 2, etc.*

118   *Now therefore thus says the Lord of hosts;*

PEOPLE, PLACES & THINGS I'D LIKE TO SEE

1 _____ ❑
2 _____ ❑
3 _____ ❑
4 _____ ❑
5 _____ ❑
6 _____ ❑
7 _____ ❑
8 _____ ❑
9 _____ ❑
10 _____ ❑
11 _____ ❑
12 _____ ❑
13 _____ ❑
14 _____ ❑
15 _____ ❑
16 _____ ❑
17 _____ ❑
18 _____ ❑
19 _____ ❑
20 _____ ❑
21 _____ ❑
22 _____ ❑
23 _____ ❑
24 _____ ❑
25 _____ ❑
26 _____ ❑
27 _____ ❑
28 _____ ❑
29 _____ ❑
30 _____ ❑
31 _____ ❑
32 _____ ❑
33 _____ ❑
34 _____ ❑
35 _____ ❑

36 _____ ❑
37 _____ ❑
38 _____ ❑
39 _____ ❑
40 _____ ❑
41 _____ ❑
42 _____ ❑
43 _____ ❑
44 _____ ❑
45 _____ ❑
46 _____ ❑
47 _____ ❑
48 _____ ❑
49 _____ ❑
50 _____ ❑
51 _____ ❑
52 _____ ❑
53 _____ ❑
54 _____ ❑
55 _____ ❑
56 _____ ❑
57 _____ ❑
58 _____ ❑
59 _____ ❑
60 _____ ❑
61 _____ ❑
62 _____ ❑
63 _____ ❑
64 _____ ❑
65 _____ ❑
66 _____ ❑
67 _____ ❑
68 _____ ❑
69 _____ ❑
70 _____ ❑

Consider your ways. Haggai 1:5

PRAYER LIST

Date	Person	Prayer Request	
			❏
			❏
			❏
			❏
			❏
			❏
			❏
			❏
			❏
			❏
			❏
			❏
			❏
			❏
			❏
			❏
			❏
			❏
			❏
			❏
			❏
			❏
			❏
			❏
			❏
			❏
			❏
			❏
			❏
			❏
			❏

The Lord is good, a strong hold in the day of trouble;

PRAYER LIST

Date	Person	Prayer Request	
			❏
			❏
			❏
			❏
			❏
			❏
			❏
			❏
			❏
			❏
			❏
			❏
			❏
			❏
			❏
			❏
			❏
			❏
			❏
			❏
			❏
			❏
			❏
			❏
			❏
			❏
			❏
			❏
			❏
			❏
			❏
			❏

and he knows them that trust in him. Nahum 1:7

THANKFUL LIST

1
2
3
4
5
6
7
8
9
10
11
12
13
14
15
16
17
18
19
20
21
22
23
24
25
26
27
28
29
30
31
32
33
34
35

36
37
38
39
40
41
42
43
44
45
46
47
48
49
50
51
52
53
54
55
56
57
58
59
60
61
62
63
64
65
66
67
68
69
70

Can two walk together,

THESE ARE A FEW OF MY FAVORITE THINGS

1 Pet(s) _____
2 Animal(s) _____
3 Most unusual pet _____
4 Bug/Critter _____
5 Car(s) _____
6 Meal _____
7 Snack _____
8 Candy _____
9 Soda _____
10 Dessert _____
11 Dairy product _____
12 Protein _____
13 Vegetable _____
14 Fruit _____
15 Hot drink _____
16 Cold drink _____
17 Childhood foods _____
18 Meal Mom/Dad made _____
19 Meal I make _____
20 Restaurant _____
21 Topic of conversation _____
22 Movie(s) _____
23 Song(s) _____
24 Book(s) _____
25 Teacher who impacted my life _____
   Why? _____
26 Mentor who impacted my life _____
   Why? _____
27 Color(s) _____
28 Artist(s) _____
29 Item to shop for _____
30 Person(s) _____
31 Beach _____
32 Vacation destination _____
33 Country _____
34 State _____

It is of the Lord's mercies that we are not consumed,

FAVORITE THINGS (Continued)

35 City _____
36 Best entertainment ever seen_____
37 Hobby _____
38 Craft _____
39 Activity _____
40 Sport(s)_____
41 Team(s)_____
42 Most rewarding volunteering_____
43 My greatest gift/skill/talent _____
44 Best advice given me _____
45 Best advice I've given_____
46 Best birthday I ever had _____
47 Most amazing natural wonder I've seen _____
48 Best road trip I've taken _____
49 Best haircut_____
50 Best gift ever given me _____
51 Best gift I ever gave another_____
52 Proudest achievement _____
53 Job _____
54 Household chore_____
55 Jewelry _____
56 Kindest thing someone did for me _____
57 Kindest things I've done for someone_____
58 Most healthy I've ever been _____
59 Perfume _____
60 Smell_____
61 Most fun I've ever had on a weekend _____
62 Favorite dance song _____
63 Favorite dance partner _____
64 Happiest moment I can recall _____
65 Hymn _____
66 Song that makes me sad _____
67 Song that makes me happy _____
68 Song that makes me want to dance _____
69 Song that annoys me _____
70 Song I like to sing_____

because his compassions fail not. Lamentations 3:22   **125**

THESE ARE A FEW OF MY FAVORITE THINGS

71 Best New Year's Eve _____

72 Best New Year's Day _____

73 Best Valentine's Day _____

74 Best Easter _____

75 Best Memorial Day _____

76 Best Mother's Day _____

77 Best Father's Day _____

78 Best 4th of July _____

79 Best Labor Day _____

80 Best Thanksgiving _____

81 Best Christmas _____

82 Biggest moment of celebrity _____
   Why?_____

83 Famous family member(s) _____

84 Favorite item of clothing _____

85 One item I can't live without _____

86 Most fun sporting event I've attended _____

87 Where I'd spend the rest of my life if I could _____

88 Memory with my husband/wife _____

89 Memory with son(s) _____

90 Memory with daughter(s) _____

91 Memory with brother(s) _____

92 Memory with sister(s) _____

93 Memory with aunt(s) _____

94 Memory with uncle(s) _____

95 Memory with Dad _____

96 Memory with Mom _____

97 Memory with Grandma(s) _____

98 Memory with Grandpa(s) _____

99 Memory with cousin(s) _____

100 Memory with non-relative _____

101 Famous person I'd like to meet _____

102 Famous person I've met _____

103 Flower/Gift delivery from _____

104 Most money I've ever made in a day/week/month _____

105 Most significant change _____

And you shall seek me, and find me,

FAVORITE THINGS (Continued)

106 Bike/Toy _____
107 Prefer ❑ Burial ❑ Cremation ❑ Other _____
Why?_____
108 Stuffed animal_____
109 Environmental sound (rain, thunder, etc) _____
110 TV show _____
111 TV rerun _____
112 Baseball Team _____
113 Poem _____
114 Picture ever taken_____
115 Fun game played _____
116 Hardest I've ever laughed_____
117 Favorite kitchen smell_____
118 Cooking smell_____
119 Weirdest thing I've ever eaten _____
120 Exercise _____
121 Beach _____
122 Football Team_____
123 Amusement Park _____
124 Other Sport/Team _____
125 Olympic Sport_____
126 Weather season _____
127 Basketball Team _____
128 Hockey Team _____
129 Mode of travel (car, bus, boat, plane, train, etc.) _____
130 Body of water (river, lake, etc.) _____
131 Camp, campsite, retreat center _____
132 Computer or phone (Apple, iPhone, PC, Android, etc.) _____
133 _____
134 _____
135 _____
136 _____
137 _____
138 _____
139 _____

when you shall search for me with all your heart. Jeremiah 29:13   **127**

THESE ARE A FEW OF MY FAVORITE THINGS

140 _____
141 _____
142 _____
143 _____
144 _____
145 _____
146 _____
147 _____
148 _____
149 _____
150 _____
151 _____
152 _____
153 _____
154 _____
155 _____
156 _____
157 _____
158 _____
159 _____
160 _____
161 _____
162 _____
163 _____
164 _____
165 _____
166 _____
167 _____
168 _____
169 _____
170 _____

To every thing there is a season,

FAVORITE THINGS (Continued)

171 _____
172 _____
173 _____
174 _____
175 _____
176 _____
177 _____
178 _____
179 _____
180 _____
181 _____
182 _____
183 _____
184 _____
185 _____
186 _____
187 _____
188 _____
189 _____
190 _____
191 _____
192 _____
193 _____
194 _____
195 _____
196 _____
197 _____
198 _____
199 _____
200 _____

and a time to every purpose under the heaven: Ecclesiastes 3:1 **129**

TO DO LIST

1 _____ ☐
2 _____ ☐
3 _____ ☐
4 _____ ☐
5 _____ ☐
6 _____ ☐
7 _____ ☐
8 _____ ☐
9 _____ ☐
10 _____ ☐
11 _____ ☐
12 _____ ☐
13 _____ ☐
14 _____ ☐
15 _____ ☐
16 _____ ☐
17 _____ ☐
18 _____ ☐
19 _____ ☐
20 _____ ☐
21 _____ ☐
22 _____ ☐
23 _____ ☐
24 _____ ☐
25 _____ ☐
26 _____ ☐
27 _____ ☐
28 _____ ☐
29 _____ ☐
30 _____ ☐
31 _____ ☐
32 _____ ☐
33 _____ ☐
34 _____ ☐
35 _____ ☐

Your word is a lamp unto my feet,

WHAT I WANT MY LOVED ONES TO KNOW ABOUT ME

and a light unto my path. Psalm 119:105

131

The Lord make his face shine upon you,

and be gracious unto you: Numbers 6:25

You shall have no other gods before me. Exodus 20:3

Help us help others (Side 1 of 2)

Share how you found this book helpful, or how God used it to affect you:

_____

_____

_____

_____

_____

_____

_____

_____

_____

_____

_____

_____

_____

_____

_____

_____

List the activities or page numbers you enjoyed the most:_____

_____

_____

Is there anything you would add to this type of book to make it better?

_____

_____

_____

Can you share a comment, complaint, idea, or suggestion?

_____

_____

_____

Tell us if you noticed an error in need of correction:

_____

_____

Note: We share letters and responses submitted to our ministry to rally prayer support for you and others. We blot out names and identifying information (unless you also sign below).

❏ I am incarcerated. I have completed this form myself and mailed it <u>directly from my institution</u>. I would appreciate a Biblically based book to keep me "Busy in The Bible"™ *(available until donations are depleted).*

First & Last Name _____

Birthplace_____ Birthdate _____

ID# or Fed A# _____ Housing/Cell _____

Facility Name _____

Facility Address _____

City/State/Zip _____

❏ Please pray for the prayer request I have included in this envelope.

In addition to social media (above): **OPTIONAL**—As an adult, I grant permission to publish, in any form, my name with all or part of my comments (this page front & back) without compensation—allowing editing as needed.

Please print legibly

✕_____
Signature   Name Printed   Date

Renewing Lives, PO Box **5529**, Diamond Bar, CA 91765-7529

Made in the USA
Monee, IL
23 May 2021